Best Bets for Babies

Best Bets for Babies

Time-saving, trouble-saving,
money-saving tips
for your baby's first two years
from the real experts—parents!

Brooke McKamy Beebe

FOREWORD BY ROSE G. AMES, M.D.

with illustrations by Denise Cavalieri Fike

A DELL TRADE PAPERBACK

A DELL TRADE PAPERBACK
Published by
Dell Publishing Co., Inc.
1 Dag Hammarskjold Plaza
New York, New York 10017

Dell ® TM 681510, Dell Publishing Co., Inc.

ISBN: 0-440-50453-8

Designed by Stanley S. Drate

Printed in the United States of America

First printing—July 1981

For Scott, my inspiration,
and
for Tyler, my support

Contents

Foreword

I enjoyed reading *Best Bets for Babies*, and I think it's a helpful and very practical book for parents. Reading it made me feel as if I were on a park bench with a group of mothers sharing practical information about babies. The hundreds of tips in this collection will help any new parent cope with some of the major and minor difficulties of babyhood.

The book is medically safe, and contains many of the tips I give to parents every day. But always use your common sense when taking anyone's advice. *You* know your child best. If you have any question at all about a course of action, ask your own doctor about it.

Babies and parents are individuals; and what I feel is so valuable about this collection is that it presents many alternative solutions to problems and not just one person's philosophy or approach. In my thirty years as a pediatrician I have seen that many different things can work for parents and babies, and my feeling always has been that if something works for you, and it's safe, it's probably fine. Trust your own instincts. Look over these tips, then decide which ones satisfy *your* needs.

I hope you enjoy this book as much as I did.

Rose G. Ames, M.D.

Acknowledgments

I'm especially grateful to Dr. Rose Ames, who checked the book for medical safety; to my editor, Sandra Choron, for her contributions as editor and mother; to Kathie du Quesnay, Maryellen Phelan, Eileen Roth Paroff, and Lisa Heila for their most welcome assistance; to Dr. Bob Seaver for his encouragement and enthusiasm right from the beginning; to my parents, Steve and Bill McKamy, for their loving support; to my husband, Tyler, who believed it could be done and helped me in countless ways to do it; and to my son, Scott, without whom I would never have known the need for such a book.

I want to take the opportunity here to thank all the people listed below, who contributed their time, energy, and experiences so generously. These are the people who really wrote the book.

Constance Aglione
Alexander Anderson
Linda Arluna
Robin Bader
Susan Barnes-Brown
Sheila Barticciotto
Laurel Bernstein

Bonnie Bick
Maggie Bitencourt
Marjory Bleier
Mary Bortz
Molli Bot
Marti Bowen
Susan Bozorsky

Pat Brosnan
Maggie Brown
Marci Burns
Randi Cambi
Cynthia Carlaw
Susan Court
Barbara Coyne

Catherine Daly
Alice DeClemente
Dick Dresner
Kathie du Quesnay
Kathleen Dymes
Fiona Edelstein
Elaine J. Eisenman
June Ekelund
Patricia C. Endreny
Laura Lee Fiore
Marian Gassman
Rhonda Gaston
Lorraine Gelardi
Shirley Glickman
Shirley Gonzales
Lynn Gorey
Maria Grande
Sandy Grant
Margaret Greiner
Nancy Gross
Gayle Hager
Barbara Hamill
Joan Hanley
Lynn A. Hanover
Karen Heckman
Barbara K. Hickernell
Vera Hirschel
Janice Hoffman
Carol Jaconetti
Kathleen Kane-Molito
Fran Kardauskas
Suzann Kettler
Kathy Kirtley
Joanne Kline

Joan M. Koenig
Bridget Krowe
Karin Krueger
Carol Krzeminski
Meghan Kvasnak
Pembroke Kyle
Christie Larned
Jill Lerner
Loretta Levinus
Ellen Lord
Cliff Lunn
Irene Lunn
Carol McGrath
Myrna Malave-Stoiber
Jeanette Malca
Marilyn Botkin Markowitz
Pat Marwell
Elaine Merker
DaLee Miller
Rosemary H. Minhas
Ronni Ellen Minsky
Mary Ann Moore
Susan Morettini
Chris Mudd
Carol Muller
Hedy Mutchnik
Annette Natarelli
Celeste Odierna
Patricia O'Keeffe
Barbara Orlowski
Dina Painter
Eileen Roth Paroff
Carolyn Parqueth
Joan Peterson-Arnold

Mark Phelan
Maryellen Phelan
Ginnie Piechicniski
Karen Presha
Abigail Rearl
Anna Reiter
Kay A. Rice
Pam Robie
Carol Rodgers
Betsy Rodino
Bunny Roosevelt
Dawn Sangrey
Susan K. Sayre
Janet Schloat
Paula Mae Schwartz
Darlene H. Shea
Lucy Sherry
Elizabeth Silverman
Ann Marie Smith
Jean Sparacin
Sandra Spitz
Laurie Sterlacci
Pamela Torborg
Eleanor P. Vail
Patricia Vail
Judy Vaillancourt
Winky Van der Hoeve
Linda Wade
Judith Werkstell
Beatrice Werner
Sally Wolfson
Alison M. Yeazel
Debra Yerys
Nadine Ziegler

Introduction

Best Bets for Babies is a collection of tips, advice, and suggestions about babies from hundreds of parents. In the three years that I have been collecting these tips from personal interviews and questionnaires, I have heard many wonderful ideas that would have been so helpful to me during those first, difficult years of motherhood.

When I brought my son, Scott, home from the hospital, I was totally unprepared for what would happen. I had thought that caring for a baby would be quite simple. Surely I could handle the fairly limited needs of an infant. Within two weeks, the reality of my situation began to sink in. I was exhausted and bewildered. I had so many questions but few answers. I tried to read and learn as much as I could about babies, but it was difficult to find the time, and although the theories about growth and development were interesting, I really needed to find practical solutions to my particular problems.

What really helped me most was talking to other parents who were going through the same thing. We'd share information about what really worked for our babies, and, to my surprise, the simple, practical tips we exchanged helped us all cope much better with the trials and traumas of babyhood.

xvii

It occurred to me that a collection of these tips would help other parents, too, and I began asking friends and friends of friends to share their ideas with me for a book. That's how *Best Bets for Babies* began.

The tips in this book are all from parents, and they have worked for the parents who offered them to me. There are no theories here; instead, I've tried to include as many varied—often contradictory—but workable ways to cope with a problem as I could. Of course, not all the tips will work for all babies. Babies are individuals, after all, and what delights one will bore another. But you never know what will work until you try it.

I remember one mother telling me that when her very placid baby cried, she'd lay him over her knees and rub his back to stop his crying. I thought to myself that it sounded like a nice idea for a quiet baby, but would never work with a more demanding, active one like mine. Well, one day, when Scott was fussing for what seemed like the tenth time that morning, I tried it. And it worked. And I knew that as simple as the idea was, I would never have thought of it myself.

Some of the ideas in this book may strike you as laughably obvious, like the one I mentioned above. But it worked—it helped me, and I pass it along on that basis with the hope that it will help someone else. Actually, I've found that the simplest suggestions often work the best, but they're usually the last thing we try.

This book is not a substitute for a supportive network of parents, who will share all your joys and frustrations and are an invaluable source of advice and comfort. Nor is it a substitute for your own very good instincts. But I hope it will provide you with many ideas that will make life with your baby easier and more fun. Keep it handy for those times when

ou've run out of your own ideas. Check it as your baby grows
nd changes; what doesn't work at three months will often
vork when the child is older. When you run into any new
ituation, see how other parents have coped with it. Check off
hose tips in the book that work for you; they'll be a handy
eference for later use. As you hear tips that seem useful, add
hem to the back of this book.

And if you'd like to share your tips, ideas, and/or
uggestions with me, I'd be delighted to receive them. (See
ne write-in information on p. 221.) This book is by parents
nd for parents, and the more input it has, the more helpful it
rill be. Please let me know if the book has been useful to
ou, for that was the whole point of writing it. I hope you
njoy it, too.

Brooke McKamy Beebe

Best Bets for Babies

1

In the Hospital

Congratulations! You have just experienced one of life's most exciting wonders. You might already have heard that things will never be the same again. In a few days, your new family will return home to have a myriad of unexpected joys—and problems. Make no mistake about it: Your questions will be endless, and your resources will be constantly challenged.

It is not too soon, while you're still in the hospital, to begin preparing for the months ahead. Use this time to rest and become acquainted with the newest member of your family. And don't be shy about ensuring that this recuperation period is as pleasant as it can be.

For Your Comfort

☐ Make sure you have all of your basic necessities with you. Ask someone to gather these for you if you don't have all of the following:

- 2–3 nightgowns (with front openings if you plan to nurse)
- A robe

1

- Slippers (These should have nonskid soles and be easy to slip into from a standing position. A slightly elevated heel will be most comfortable while you're healing.)
- Six pairs of underpants
- 2–3 nursing bras and nursing pads (if you intend to breast-feed)
- Toothbrush, toothpaste, shampoo, and necessary toiletries
- Makeup
- A shower cap (if you use one)
- Any hair-setting device that will make it easy for you to look your best
- A few dollars for newspapers, magazines, and sundries.

☐ Make your hospital room as homey as possible. Consider bringing some of the following things from home:

- Photos of family, especially other children
- A portable tape recorder with your favorite tapes, or just a music box. (Be sure to share these with your baby.)
- A small clock with an alarm
- Any luxuries you might enjoy, like scented soap or perfumed candles
- A lighted mirror for makeup
- Hangers for special nightclothes and your going-home outfit.

☐ These might come in handy, too:

- Your address book with phone numbers
- Stationery for thank-you notes
- A manicure kit

- A notebook and pen for recording questions and their answers. Use it for jotting down your feelings and impressions, too.
- Books about babies
- Books about nursing and the phone number of the local LaLeche League counselor.

☐ Pillows from home are much more comfortable for you and baby. Be sure to use a plastic covering—under the pillowcase—if you're going to rest the baby on them.

☐ Have your husband bring cake or special treats for the nurses. Or pass on your surplus of flowers. It *really* makes a difference! The nurses will be special to you in return.

☐ If you hate the hospital food, have someone bring your favorite foods in. (This is the perfect time for a romantic, uninterrupted champagne dinner shared by you and your husband. It may be your last for a while!)

☐ Close your door if the noise bothers you. There's no rule against it. Make use of the "Do Not Disturb" sign if there is one. If there isn't, make your own. You might want to explain to the nurse why you put the sign up.

☐ Have the switchboard hold all calls while you're resting or spending time with your new baby.

☐ Try running the hot water in the shower full blast for a few moments, then relax in the bathroom for an instant steam bath.

Doctors' Visits

☐ Write down your questions during the day as you think of them and have them handy when the doctor walks in. Don't forget to write down the answers.

☐ Have your obstetrician/gynecologist or a member of the hospital staff recommend a pediatrician if you haven't already chosen one. Try to make contact with him or her before you leave the hospital. If possible, arrange to have your own pediatrician examine your baby before you go home. (See PEDIATRICIANS, p. 199, for information on how to choose one.)

☐ If the pediatrician or ob/gyn are too rushed to answer all your questions on their rounds, call them at their offices. You need and deserve complete and thoughtful answers to your questions.

Hospital Regulations

You have got to be very tough and *insist* on your rights in the hospital. Be nice but firm. If you have difficulties with the nurses, ask to see the head nurse. Tell your doctors about any problems. If this doesn't do any good, get someone else, like your husband, to do it for you. (No matter how firm and decisive you may be at home or at work, the birth experience can leave you emotionally and physically exhausted. It's often hard to challenge anything in this state. So accept help if you need it.)

☐ If you're having trouble with hospital regulations, get your doctor or pediatrician to leave specific written instructions about what you want.

☐ Try to anticipate your needs (sleeping pills, etc.) so that you can request them in advance and avoid having to wait for them later on.

☐ If they send in a bottle of sugar water for the baby but you requested plain water, buzz the nursery and make them replace it. Keep this up and they'll soon learn.

☐ Pain-killers can make you depressed. They also slow down your intestinal activity, causing distension and that uncomfortable "gassy" feeling. If this happens, stop taking them. You have the right.

☐ Discuss any and all problems with your doctor. Remember that you have a certain set of rights as an obstetric patient, according to the American Hospital Association. They are as follow:

- The right to participate in all decisions that affect the well-being of you and your baby unless a medical emergency is involved
- The right to be informed of the risks, hazards, or side effects of any drugs that are administered to you or your child
- The right to be informed of which drugs are being administered and the right to refuse them
- The right to know the names and qualifications of individuals prescribing medications involved in your care and that of your child
- The right to be informed about any procedures that are being administered to you and your child
- The right to be accompanied at any time during labor and birth by someone to whom you look for emotional support
- The right to have your baby cared for at your bedside if your baby is normal and to feed your baby according to his or her needs
- The right to be informed about any abnormal conditions concerning you or your baby

- The right to examine all hospital records concerning you or your baby and to have copies made at a reasonable fee.

Visitors

Some mothers said visits boosted their morale, but most wished they had not had any (other than family, that is). All agreed that visits should be *limited*—anywhere from fifteen minutes to an hour.

☐ Save your fancy nightgowns for visiting hours. The hospital gowns will serve you well the rest of the time.

☐ If your roommate really bothers you by talking too much or having too many visitors, tell the nurse about it and ask to be moved. Don't be shy. She'll usually try to accommodate, and you do need your rest.

☐ Be firm about telling visitors to stay away if you don't care to see them. Suggest that they wait until you're all settled at home before they visit.

☐ Although visitors and callers will request detailed, blow-by-blow descriptions of the birth, you'll have more time for yourself if you keep these discussions general.

☐ If you're a working mother, consider the pros and cons of inviting office staff to visit you in the hospital. Some women are happy to see old faces; it makes others feel "left out."

☐ Send baby gifts home with your husband, so you'll have that much less to carry on your last day in the hospital.

☐ Keep a list of presents and the people who gave them to you.

Night Feedings

Nursing mothers felt that night feedings were necessary for establishing the milk supply. Mothers whose babies were bottle fed often advised getting the rest instead. Here are two interesting points of view:

"The nurses always talked me out of the night feedings each night and I was sorry. I couldn't sleep well anyway (in part due to worrying if the baby was crying), and I wish I'd tried them. If they had worn me out, then I could have stopped them. What I'm trying to say is, if you're game, then try. If the feedings do exhaust you, you can always decide to skip them."

"Don't pamper yourself too much. It's tempting to sleep through the night (especially with older children at home), but sometimes you've really got to work to make a baby eat, and a nurse might not take the time. It really depends on how your baby is doing."

Recording the Event

☐ Be sure to record those first days in the hospital in pictures. Both you and your husband should learn to use the camera before baby's arrival. Be sure to get a nurse or a visitor to take a few pictures of the three of you.

☐ Avoid flash attachments if possible. Shooting with available light preserves the moment and the atmosphere in a less artificial way. Anyway, hospital rooms are usually very well lit.

☐ *Never* mail the pictures of the birth or even let them out of your sight if you don't have negatives or duplicates. They might get lost, and, obviously, they're irreplaceable.

☐ Keep a spare roll of film in the hospital so you won't be caught without.

☐ When taking portrait photos of the baby, make sure you're shooting against a plain, soft-colored background, such as a light-blue blanket. Aim for a contrast that will enhance rather than interfere with the mood.

☐ Start collecting artifacts for your baby's memory book while you're still in the hospital. The following make nice additions:

- Copies of those first footprints and handprints (the hospital usually supplies these on request)
- Baby's hospital bracelet and yours
- The first photo
- Baby's hospital ID card
- A pressed flower from your favorite bouquet
- A special card or note from a loved one
- A lock of baby's hair, if she or he has any
- The tiny cap baby wears for the first few days
- Notes on visitors: what they said, what gifts they brought

☐ Get someone to pick up a newspaper on the day of baby's birth and keep it well preserved. It will be a most interesting gift when your child is grown.

☐ For more tips on preserving special moments, see pp. 214–215.

Episiotomy

Waiting for your episiotomy to heal may seem almost as trying as the birth itself, but it does help to have patience and remember that it's all for a great cause. The following tips have proved helpful:

☐ Lean over in the shower and let the warm water run over your stitches.

☐ Ask for an "ice glove" (a rubber glove with crushed ice and water in it) and apply it to your stitches in the recovery room and for several days after.

☐ Use premoistened pads (like Tucks). Keep them by the window or anyplace that's cool. The cooler they are, the better they feel. Follow the package directions.

☐ Apply heat. Ask for a heating lamp, or use a sitz bath.

☐ Apply witch hazel on small sterile pads.

☐ Spray on a local anesthetic.

☐ Avoid constipation. Eat plenty of fresh fruit and roughage and drink lots of liquids—especially prune juice. Use a stool softener if necessary.

☐ Do the Kegel exercises (slowly tighten the muscles around the vagina and anus, then release). Repeat as often as you can.

☐ Don't slump when you sit, and be sure to sit on top of the stitches, not sideways.

☐ Get a foam rubber pillow to sit on.

☐ Move around as much as you can, even if it's painful a first. If you don't move, the tissues will get stiff around th stitches and will pull painfully when you do move.

☐ Rinse the perineum after urinating or having a bowe movement. Buy a plastic squirt bottle for this purpose i the hospital has not supplied one for you.

Hemorrhoids

☐ Use premoistened pads (like Tucks). Keep them cool i you can. At home, put them in the refrigerator. Leave th pad on the hemorrhoids as long as it feels good; the change to a cooler one.

☐ Witch hazel is soothing. Apply on small sterile pads.

☐ Take a sitz bath as often as you can. Or, at home, you cai just use the bathtub.

☐ Avoid constipation by eating lots of fruit and othe high-fiber foods. Use stool-softening pills and supposi tories as needed.

☐ Codeine can be constipating. Try a local anestheti instead for relieving pain.

☐ A simple hemorrhoid operation after delivery can relieve the agony. Ask your doctor about it.

Cesarean Birth

If you were in labor and then had a Cesarean birth, it's no unusual to feel somewhat of a failure at the birthing process. Many women feel quite depressed about it. One mother told me, *"It took me a long time of questioning myself, cross-examining my doctor, and checking in medical books to understand that my first child (a transverse breech—laying across my womb) would never have been delivered alive vaginally. I had to learn to feel that rather than being unsuccessful at vaginal delivery I had been a success at coming through a C-section with a beautiful baby girl!"*

☐ Don't expect to keep up with friends who have had vaginal deliveries. You won't shrink back to normal size as quickly as they will, and your recovery will be somewhat slower, because you have undergone *major* surgery. Pamper yourself, and let others pamper you!

☐ If you plan on nursing, let the surgeon know. Medication should not be prescribed that will prevent nursing (unless it is absolutely necessary for your health).

☐ For gas pain:

- Get out of bed as soon as you can. You won't want to, but it's necessary. You've got to move around. It really helps relieve the gas and ease the pain of the stitches.
- When you're lying in bed, remember to roll from side to side every ten or fifteen minutes to help move the gas.
- A suppository works better than pills.
- Eat standing up the day after your section.
- Don't drink carbonated beverages.
- Don't use drinking straws.
- Bend over to let the gas float up and out.
- Ask the nurse for a rectal tube. One mother reported that after her first cesarean, the nurses inserted a rectal tube on a regular basis to relieve the gas, and

she never had any gas pain. But for her second and third births, she had to ask for the tube, since they didn't use it as a matter of course.

☐ Constipation is more common after C-sections; if it becomes a problem, have someone bring in a large bottle of prune juice. The nurses can refrigerate it. Drink lots until it's effective. It beats enemas!

☐ After a C-section, it's very painful to wear belts and pads. Use very large cotton underpants and beltless pads, which are much more comfortable.

☐ Before urinating, moving your bowels, sneezing, or coughing, press the incision with your hand. Pressing hard relieves the pain when you move.

☐ A folded sheet is a better incision-holder (when walking) than the pillow the nurses recommend. It's much less clumsy.

☐ If you're on medication and they won't let you have your baby, find out what the medication is and tell them to stop it if possible. It might be nothing more than a painkiller that is easily discontinued.

☐ You'll be given painkillers for as long as you want, but you'll feel much better as soon as you stop taking them. Don't take them longer than the first twenty-four hours after surgery. The discomfort is not unbearable.

☐ If you're nursing after a Cesarean, it helps to rest the baby on a couple of pillows in your lap.

☐ Lie down when you nurse. (You'll have to get the hang of this!)

☐ Have the nurses move the IV if you find it very hard to nurse. Some people prefer the hand; others find the IV in the arm most comfortable.

☐ Fevers after a Cesarean are common. Drink as much water as you humanly can to drive the fever down—it works. This prevents the hospital from enforcing their policy of removing the baby for twenty-four hours if the mother's fever is high.

☐ Ask for any literature the hospital might have on Cesareans. Nurses and doctors often forget to tell you that information is available.

☐ Hospital rules can sometimes be more flexible than you might imagine. If you have older children who may be worried about you because of the prolonged hospital stay after a C-section, a carefully worded request to the nursing supervisor should result in a meeting between you and the children in one of the hospital solariums.

☐ Remember, it's never too late to ask your doctor any questions about your Cesarean.

☐ Locate a Cesarean discussion group to share your feelings and get answers to your questions. If you can't find one, contact:

> Cesareans / Support Education and Concern
> 66 Christopher Road
> Waltham, MA 02154
> (617)547-7188

This national organization has a listing of support groups around the country. For the $8 annual membership fee, you will receive discounts on publications and a quarterly news-letter.

> The Cesarean Connection
> P.O. Box 11
> Westmont, Illinois 60559
> (312) 968-8933

For 25 cents plus a self-addressed, stamped envelope, you'll receive a sample copy of the monthly newsletter. For 50 cents plus a self-addressed stamped envelope they will send a copy of "Cesarean Childbirth Education Aids Guide," a listing of books, pamphlets, movies, etc., on Cesareans. As a member, you can also use their referral service to find a support group in your area.

☐ VBAC (Vaginal Birth After Cesarean) offers written material as well as classes and counseling on how to avoid Cesareans and repeat Cesareans. For more information send $1 to cover reprint cost and a #10 self-addressed, stamped envelope and two 15-cent stamps to:

> Nancy Wainer Cohen
> 10 Great Plain Terrace
> Neeham, Massachusetts 02192

Going Home

☐ There are many things the hospital will throw away after you leave, so ask if you can take:

- Rectal thermometer (used for baby)
- Oral thermometer (used by you)
- Foam donut (for sitting)
- Nasal syringe for baby (ask nurses to show you how to use it)

- Peri bottle (the plastic bottle with the nozzle used for cleaning after voiding)
- Chux (the disposable pads with the plastic back used for keeping blood off the sheets)
- Baby's brush or comb
- Baby's soap dish
- Baby's cap
- Baby's corrugated cardboard bassinet
- Sanitary napkins
- Tucks
- Plastic wash basin or sitz bath

☐ Have someone check you out of the hospital before you're actually ready to leave. This way, you won't be stuck filling out forms during those last hectic moments.

☐ If you have hired a nurse to help you at home, consider having her meet you at the hospital before you leave, unless you'd rather have some time at home alone first.

☐ If you think it will make you feel better, ask someone to put the finishing touches on the baby's room before you leave for home. Many mothers reported that having that job out of the way made the hospital stay so much more relaxing.

☐ If there are other children at home, let them participate in your homecoming by choosing baby's outfit for the trip home.

☐ Try to have all last-minute shopping for baby out of the way upon your arrival home. The following should start you off right. A more detailed discussion of these items may be found in Chapter 3, "Clothes and Laundry" and Chapter 4, "Furniture and Accessories."

- 6 undershirts (3 month size)
- 10–12 stretch suits (three-month size)
- 3–4 drawstring nightgowns or kimonos (for summer babies only)
- 2 receiving blankets
- 4–6 dozen cloth diapers or 2 boxes of newborn-size disposable diapers
- 12 cloth diapers (Even if you're using disposables, these have all sorts of uses!)
- A sweater
- A hat
- A bunting or snowsuit (for cold-weather babies)
- 3 baby towels
- A diaper pail (This is supplied to you if you use a diaper service.)
- A changing table
- A crib or bassinet for baby to sleep in
- Waterproof mattress covers for the crib (Get these in two sizes—one to cover the entire mattress and smaller ones to place over the larger ones in strategic places so that you needn't change the entire covering when only a small section is soiled. If you can't find the smaller size covers, cut up a few large ones.)
- 4 fitted sheets
- A padded crib bumper
- 2 blankets or quilts (for cold-weather babies)
- A carriage or stroller
- 1 pacifier (See if the baby likes it before you buy others.)
- A rectal thermometer
- Baby powder
- Baby lotion
- Petroleum jelly

- Diaper rash ointment
- Nail scissors
- Baby shampoo
- Mild bar soap, such as Ivory
- A car seat
- A cloth baby carrier
- An infant seat.

☐ You'll also need the following feeding supplies for bottle-fed babies:

- 8–10 glass or plastic bottles with collars, discs, and caps
- 12 nipples
- A bottle brush
- A nipple brush
- A measuring cup with spout
- A long-handled spoon
- A bottle sterilizer (or a large pot for holding bottles)
- Tongs
- A two-day supply of formula (The hospital sometimes supplies this).

General Observations

☐ If you have a baby boy and have decided to have him circumcised, you might want to remember to undress him as soon as you can after delivery so you can see him uncircumcised.

☐ Undress your baby anytime you want. Don't be intimidated by all that tight, precise wrapping.

☐ Private rooms are delightful and a real luxury if you can get them. But you can get very lonely in the hospital.

Take lots of walks to the nursery and introduce yourself to the other mothers. You've just had an incredible experience and so have they. Everyone wants to share it, so don't be shy.

☐ Ask the nurse to demonstrate techniques for diapering, bathing, swaddling, burping, etc.

☐ Try your own homecoming clothes on *before* you go home. You may find you need something looser.

☐ Make sure you ask the nurses if they have classes for new mothers. Nurses often forget to mention these.

☐ The International Childbirth Education Association (ICEA) endeavors to join together people interested in family-centered maternity and infant care. Write to them to find the ICEA group nearest you. Member groups are autonomous and offer many different services. They also offer a list of parent-oriented publications. The address is

ICEA
P.O. Box 20048
Minneapolis, MN 55420

☐ If you have twins, contact:
National Organization of Mothers-of-Twins Club, Inc.
5402 Amberwood Lane
Rockville, Maryland 20853 or call(301) 460-9108.
They will send you a pamphlet of helpful hints and the address of the nearest club affiliate. A quarterly newspaper bulletin is available for $5 a year.

☐ If your baby is premature, it is really worth it to do whatever you can to get the hospital to allow your other children to see him *in* the hospital. Says one mother, *"My children weren't scared at all by the tubes and needles. Of course, I had prepared them for what to expect. That visit to the baby reassured them tremendously, and helped them understand what was going on."*

2

The First Weeks At Home

The first weeks at home can be very difficult. Whether you're a first-time mother or are having your sixth child, you're going to have a period of adjustment.

Fortunately, most of the problems that develop in the first few weeks are easily solved, but it might not seem so at the time. I hope this chapter will help you make an easy adjustment to your new life.

Help at Home

Some kind of help is necessary after you come home from the hospital. Here are some choices.

HIRED HELP

☐ There are many ways to contact hired help, and it's best to do this before the baby arrives. But if you haven't been able to plan in advance, or if you planned on doing it all yourself and then changed your mind, remember that it's never too late to find someone. The following methods can be employed to locate help:

- Contact friends who were satisfied with the people they used.
- Ask store owners in your community to recommend someone.
- Place an ad in the local newspaper or shopper.
- Contact your local senior-citizen center.
- Approach church and temple groups.
- If there is a college in your area, call the placement office. (Or try the Home Economics department of a nearby high school.)
- Call a local state employment agency.
- Work through a professional agency; see the Yellow Pages entry for "Nurses" and "Sitting Services."
- Call local preschool nurseries.
- Check to see whether your hospital has a referral service.

☐ Ask for references and check them. If you're told to call at a specific time, be sure *not* to call at that time. (It may be a "setup," with a phony reference standing by for your call.)

☐ A housekeeper is more useful than a baby nurse. Some baby nurses will only care for the baby and you might want to concentrate on doing that yourself.

☐ Be specific about the duties you want your household help to perform. Clarify these during the interview. Prepare a list so that there are no misunderstandings. Consider some or all of the following:

- Caring for the new baby
- Preparing meals for all members of the family
- Laundry (baby's and yours)
- Answering the telephone

- Greeting guests
- Preparing snacks for visitors
- Kitchen cleanup
- Dusting and light housekeeping (specify all duties)
- Watering plants
- Getting other children off to school
- Shopping.

☐ Remember that having a nurse in the house means another person to cook for—unless you've made cooking part of the nurse's duties.

☐ If you're hiring a nurse to help you with the baby, make sure you, your husband, and your other children can get along with her. You'll be seeing a lot of each other.

☐ Avoid nurses who talk too much. (You can generally spot this tendency in an interview.)

☐ Remember that a nurse is not a substitute mother; don't let her take over completely if you feel up to pitching in. Practice saying "I'd like to do that myself!"

☐ Even if you've hired a nurse for two weeks, don't be shy about asking her to leave after two days if you'd rather be on your own. Or if you've hired someone through an agency and would like a replacement for any reason at all, go ahead and request it. The agency will explain it to the nurse.

☐ Most communities have a Visiting Nurse Service, which will send a nurse to your home, sometimes free of charge, to show you how to do various baby-related tasks like bathing the baby. The service will also answer any questions you might have. But these are brief visits; if you need full-time nursing help, the service can tell you where to look for it. You can get in touch with the service through your state or county public health departments; or consult your telephone directory.

☐ Make use of baby-sitters, who can take older children out for an afternoon or come by just to help with some of the household chores.

FAMILY HELP

☐ Consider asking family members to come by on a rotating schedule to help out.

☐ Even if you don't get along with your mother or mother-in-law, don't categorically refuse her offer to help with the baby. You might find that one of your strongest needs at this time is to be mothered. Leave your options open, so if you need her you can ask her.

☐ Don't overlook the small jobs that even the youngest members of your household can perform. (See SIBLINGS: STARTING OUT RIGHT, p. 25.)

HUSBAND HELP: PERSONAL EXPERIENCES

"My husband stayed home for a week after the baby was born in order to help me, but once the baby's needs were taken care of, he used the time to work around the house. I began to get lonely and then angry at being left alone. It was months before I talked to him about it and I realized that he had no idea how I felt, even though it seemed so obvious that I needed comforting and caring company."

"If your husband is staying with you to help after the baby is born, don't expect too much help unless he has already proven to be a terrific cook and housekeeper. My husband really did not know how too take care of the house and me, because he'd never really done it before, and—it's funny—it never occurred to me that he wouldn't really know what to do."

"Having my husband home with me was the best tonic I could have had. He made me stay in bed for three days and took care of everything."

"How did I get my husband to make dinner every night after I came home from the hospital? I just asked him. Try it."

Siblings: Starting Out Right

☐ Never walk in carrying the new arrival. Always be free to greet the older child.

☐ Involve the older child in the baby's life right from the beginning. Have him select the homecoming outfit, ask him to help strap baby into the car seat on the way home from the hospital, etc. Remember, you are helping to form a lifetime relationship, and if you can make an older sibling feel good about the new baby, you are helping to lay the groundwork for a smoother relationship.

☐ Try this for your homecoming: Arrange to have your older children out of the house when you come home with the baby, so you two can settle in and relax (and you can adjust to your new role as the mother of one more). Then you can focus all your love and attention on the older children when you first see them.

☐ One mother reported, *"When we went to pick up our adopted baby, we had a neighbor sneak a new guinea pig into our four-year-old son's room. Once we returned, we had flocks of friends come over—many of them with preschoolers. The guinea pig made the day special for Paul, and he, too, had something to show off to his friends, who were also indifferent to the baby. This left more time for the adults to fuss and flatter."*

☐ Don't be surprised if your other child is very cool to the new baby. It's often been said that if you want to know how the child feels, imagine how *you* would feel if your husband brought home a new wife and tried to convince you what a good idea it was.

☐ Ask friends and relatives to pay attention to the other child, too, when they come to visit. This is most important. And it doesn't hurt to have a few small toys to give the child when people bring gifts for the baby.

☐ Always refer to the new little one as "our" baby.

☐ As you're changing, feeding, or playing with the baby, tell the older one(s) how much you fussed over them when they were babies.

☐ Thank them often for being so good to the new baby. Stress the fact that it's nice to have a helper now.

☐ Give the older child a new doll when baby comes home as his own baby. Don't be surprised if it gets some pretty rough treatment.

☐ Keep a step stool next to the changing table so that little ones can watch and help.

☐ Have juice and a snack ready for the older child when you're feeding the baby. Welcome her on your lap, too, for reading or just talking.

☐ Occasionally give the older child presents "from" the baby.

☐ Try to spend some time alone with the older child every day doing something she really enjoys.

☐ Emphasize the older child's "seniority" by giving her new privileges: sleeping in a larger bed, a new place at the dinner table, the responsibility of setting the table, use of the telephone (with help), or an advanced toy.

☐ Be sure to explain to older children that the new baby "can't do anything yet." Toddlers often interpret an infant's lack of speech and playfulness as hostility.

☐ Try reading any of the following books (or others that you may find on the subject) to the older child:

> *We Got This New Baby at Our House* by Janet Sinberg, illustrated by Nancy Gray (New York: Avon, 1980).
> *Nobody Asked* Me *If I Wanted a Baby Sister* by Martha Alexander (New York: Dial, 1971).
> *The New Baby* by Ruth and Harold Shane, illustrated by Eloise Wilkin (Racine, Wisconsin: Western Publishing, 1979).

Taking It Easy

You'll save yourself a world of problems if you take things slowly in the beginning. Avoid the "supermon syndrome"; just face the fact that you can't do everything you used to do *and* care for a baby. The following tips may help.

☐ Learn to let things go—don't be a stickler about the housekeeping. In a very short time you *will* have time to take a bath, you *will* wash your hair more often, things *will* (more or less) get back to normal. It doesn't seem possible now, but it does happen.

☐ If you have a telephone answering machine, record the details of the birth on it for your friends and let it talk to them for a few days while you rest. Or just turn it on during baby's nap time (and yours).

☐ Ask your husband to bring you breakfast in bed before he leaves for work. Being able to rest in the morning can get you through the day, especially if you've been up all night.

☐ If your husband can take one of the night feedings, the extra rest will speed your recuperation.

☐ If the baby's nightly sighs and stirs keep you awake at night, move her out of your bedroom. If she really needs you, she'll let you know.

☐ Why add food shopping to your chores? Splurge for a few weeks and find a store that will deliver your groceries.

☐ Send out for meals for a few days.

☐ Use paper plates.

☐ Get into the habit of sleeping during baby's naps.

☐ Keep a thermos of milk or juice and a bowl of fresh fruit, peanuts, raisins, or prepackaged cheese chunks next to your bed (or wherever you spend most of your time) for instant nourishment. It's a lot easier to recuperate if you're well nourished.

☐ Feed baby in bed with the older sibling reading alongside (or being read to). With luck, you'll all fall asleep for a good nap.

☐ Throw some milk and a banana into the blender for a quick, nutritious, filling pickup.

☐ *Make* yourself go out alone with your husband and your friends, even if it's just for an hour or so. Even if you don't *feel* like going out, it will feel great once you do it.

☐ Take a walk with the baby as soon as you can. It gives you a feeling of freedom and cleanses your mind and your vision.

☐ Take baby out right after a feeding to maximize the chances that baby will be in a good mood while you're out.

☐ If you've hired a live-in nurse, take advantage of your freedom. Spend an evening out with your husband as soon as you're feeling up to it.

☐ Try to arrange to have someone care for the baby while you do something just for yourself:
  • A visit to the hairdresser (Consider a new, shorter hairstyle.)
  • A manicure

- A pedicure
- A facial
- A few hours at a health spa
- A long walk
- A matinee
- Lunch with a friend at your favorite restaurant
- A shopping trip to buy something special—just for you
- A luxurious bubble bath
- Reading a book—not one on childcare!
- Calling or seeing a friend—and *don't* talk about the baby!
- If you were working before the baby came, a visit to the office.

Postpartum Problems

Postpartum problems can be caused by the great amount of changing hormonal activity that your body is experiencing at this time, or it can be the result of fatigue, improper nutrition, or an overwhelming reaction to new responsibilities. These feelings can occur immediately after the pregnancy or as much as a year after the birth. Mothers of adopted children often have them, too. Be sure to check with your doctor if you feel that something is seriously wrong, especially if you are taking any medication. Do be sure that you're getting a balanced diet, and find some postpartum exercises that will help you get back in shape. Looking good *will* make you feel better! Mothers interviewed almost unanimously pointed out that talking about their real feelings helped to alleviate pressures.

Learn to relax—and learn how to ask for help. Here are some guidelines:

☐ Talk to other mothers. (See pp. 32–33 for information on how to join a mother's group.)

☐ If you're exhausted, let the house go, let visitors go, and just sleep as much as you can. Make it a top priority, at least for a few days.

☐ Ask your husband for help with daily chores, nighttime feedings, or whatever chore you simply can't face. Can he take off a few days or afternoons? It also helps to establish a fixed time period, like Sunday morning, that is always *your* time to be alone. Work this out with your spouse. It might be all you need.

☐ If you want your husband to do more of the work, learn to tell him specifically what you need. Rather than saying "You're not helping enough," try "Will you please bathe the baby while I get dressed?"

☐ If friends and relatives can't help with the work load, hire someone.

☐ If you are taking pain killers, stop. They can make you feel depressed.

☐ Go ahead and cry!

☐ Tell your baby how you feel! Remember, you can say *anything* you want to, as long as you say it nicely.

☐ Get as far away from the baby as you can and yell about all the things that are bothering you.

☐ Try a physical activity like running or jumping rope. It really helps to dissipate anger and frustration.

☐ Brewer's yeast in fruit juice is a good pickup. If you can't stand the taste, hold your nose. Or try antistress vitamin pills that have plenty of C and B vitamins.

☐ Make sure you eat regularly and nutritiously. *Don't* snack on junk food.

☐ If you can't sleep at night, do some stretching exercises before bedtime or take a warm bath. A glass of wine will help, too.

☐ Tell your ob/gyn how you feel; don't hesitate to get psychiatric help if you feel you need it. One mother we talked with offered a third alternative: *"Joint therapy worked for my husband and me. It helped my husband understand what I was going through, and with help we were able to work things out together that we had not been able to discuss rationally before."*

☐ If you're lonely, join a post-partum exercise class. You'll get back in shape and meet new friends. Or just go to a playground. You're sure to see other mothers there.

☐ Ever get frustrated when days go by and nothing seems to get done? You will feel *much* better if you set one simple task for yourself per day, and do it, no matter what.

☐ If you're feeling unattractive, focus on something you can change quickly, like a new hairstyle. Also, don't fall into the habit of wearing old clothes just because they're comfortable; wear things that make you feel attractive.

☐ Join a women's group that will enable you to share your feelings and meet new people. To find one:

   • Call your pediatrician or ob/gyn. The nurses might know of one, too.

- Ask a Lamaze instructor. Your ob/gyn will probably know of one.
- Call a local hospital.
- Ask your local YWCA or YWHA or community center.
- Start one yourself!
- Call or write to:

  ASPO (American Society for
    Psychoprophylaxis in Obstetrics)
  1411 K Street NW
  Washington, D.C. 20005
  (202) 783-7050.

They will put you in touch with a local chapter or group in your area. Many of these chapters offer "Mothers Are People, Too," a program that gives personal support to new mothers.

- Contact ICEA (International Childbirth Education Association) see p. 18
- Contact National Organization of Mothers-of-Twins Club, see p. 18
- Contact C/SEC (Cesarean/Support Education and Concern), see p. 13
- Contact The Cesarean Connection, see p. 14
- Contact The La Leche League, see p. 78

Premature Babies

☐ Your doctor will tell you how frequently to feed your baby, but it is your job to wake her up and keep her awake. Try:

- Changing her right before a feeding.

- Bathing her before a feeding.
- Undressing her so she's *slightly* cool.
- Pulling her earlobes gently or softly flicking her feet.
- Pressing your finger on one cheek. She'll turn toward your finger and open her mouth.
- Making noises (coughing, etc.)

☐ Often their sucking instinct is not strong. A pacifier helps build up their sucking strength.

☐ There are special nipples for premature babies that are good at first, but throw them away as soon as possible so baby can learn to suck more strongly.

☐ Preemies have an even harder time regulating their body temperatures than full term babies. Be *very* careful to keep temperatures evenly warm.

☐ Sometimes the extra iron in their diets can cause constipation. Ask your doctor if you can start giving the baby fruit if this occurs.

☐ Do *not* overfeed.

☐ If you want to learn more about premature babies, read only the most up-to-date information. Older books can make dire predictions that are simply not true today with the medical advances of recent years.

☐ *Don't* treat them as if they were made of glass. One mother shared the following experience: *"My four-year-old still thinks the world revolves around her, because I sheltered her, protected her and really allowed her to become spoiled. She was three months premature, but she's the strongest and smartest of my three children."*

Visitors

Many parents wished that they had not had visitors for the first week at home. Here are some suggestions for making visits easier.

☐ Tell your friends that the best visiting time for you is and that a short visit would be appreciated. Promise a longer visit later on, when you're feeling up to it.

☐ *"Visitors always seemed to come just when I'd gotten the baby to sleep and I was ready to nap,"* one mother said. *"I finally put a sign on my door that said, 'We're sleeping. Please let me know who dropped by and I'll give you a call later.' Leave a pad and pencil next to the door."*

☐ Order food in when people come to dinner. Everyone will understand. Or make it clear that only snacks will be served.

☐ Have a baby-sitter come to your home when you have guests for dinner. You'll be more relaxed if you don't have to constantly listen for baby.

☐ Small children who come visiting with their parents will be delighted to try out all of the baby's new toys—if you let them. Keep one or two toys available just for them and firmly ask their parents to control them.

☐ Everyone wants to hold the baby, especially youngsters. But it is not a good idea for her to be passed around and exposed to possible infection. Tell children that the *baby* has a cold and you don't want *them* to catch it. Keep surgical masks around for visitors to wear when they handle the baby. Blame the pediatrician for the rules if you must!

☐ Ask people with colds to stay away. Even if the baby can't catch it, *you* might, and that's the last thing you need right now. Be firm on this issue.

☐ Think of close friends as short-term baby-sitters. They can stay with the baby for a short time while you go off to take a shower, wash you hair, or catch up on some other quick chore.

☐ Give visitors waterproof pads for their laps as they handle the baby so their clothes don't get ruined.

Babies and Pets

☐ Let your dog or cat into the nursery to sniff around as you're getting it ready for the baby. Then, when baby comes home from the hospital, have someone else carry her in and be free to greet the pet. Carefully supervise the first meeting of baby and pet. Hold baby and let your pet sniff her all over.

☐ *Always* supervise when animals and babies are together. Set rules for both and enforce them.

☐ Give animals as much attention as you give baby and there should be no trouble with jealousy.

☐ Use a gate at the door to the nursery to keep pets out.

Two Ways to Carry Infants

☐ The football carry: Put baby's back along your arm and hold the head in your hand.

☐ The hip carry: Rest baby's fanny on your hip and slip your hand under the stomach. (See illustration on the opposite page.)

The Hip Carry

General Observations

☐ When you want baby to get used to something, like a car seat or pacifier, introduce it into his life as soon as possible. Remember, the younger the baby, the more adaptable he will be.

☐ Encourage Dad to spend some time alone with the baby every day—and give him lots of support.

☐ Make a mobile out of the birth cards you receive and hang it over the crib, out of baby's reach. The cards can be changed or rotated every few weeks so that there is always something new for her to look at.

☐ Don't expect flowers for the second baby. Says one mother: *"I was fussed over when the first came along, but the arrival of Number Two was greeted with nonchalance from my husband on down."* Oh, well.

☐ Check with your doctor to find out when sexual intercourse may be resumed. If intercourse is painful, try a lubricating jelly, such as K-Y. It's normal for your vagina to be very dry after birth—even if you've had a C-section. It has to do with your hormones.

☐ If intercourse continues to be painful and it seems to be internal rather than lack of lubrication, consult your ob/gyn. Don't let him or her tell you it's all in your mind. A local anesthetic may be what you need, but ask your doctor first.

Free Things for Parents

The following brochures, pamplets, and magazines dealing with newborns are free for the asking:

A six-month subscription to *American Baby* and a copy of "The First Year of Life" from:

> *American Baby* Magazine
> 575 Lexington Avenue
> New York, New York 10022

nformation about books, movies, and articles concerned
ith being a parent from:
    Parenting Materials Information Center
    Early Childhood Division
    Southwest Educational Development Laboratory
    211 East 7th Street
    Austin, Texas 78701

nformation on your child's first year from:
    Association for Childhood Educational International
    3615 Wisconsin Avenue N.W.
    Washington, D.C. 20016

3
Clothes and Laundry

Buying Clothes

☐ See the layette list on p. 16. These should get you through the first three months at least. After that, you can play it by ear. Consider also the following two opinions:

"By the third child, I found that the less baby clothes I had, the easier it was. I do more washes for the whole family anyway, and the fewer clothes I have, the less I have to sort, iron, fold, and put away."

"It was helpful to me to have a lot of baby clothes the first year so that I didn't have to wash them often. It seems more time efficient to me to do lots of laundry at once, rather than dribs and drabs throughout the week."

☐ Check the following suggestions for buying clothes in general—new or used. Avoid:

- Clothes that go over the head—babies hate them and they make dressing difficult.

- Clothes that button in the back—it's easier not to have to turn the baby over to do all the fastening.
- Clothes that have no opening at the bottom for diaper changes.
- Newborn/layette sizes. Invest in three- to six-month sizes instead; you'll be needing them sooner than you think.
- Booties—they don't stay on. Get socks with good elastic at the top (Eddy, Humpty Dumpty) that can't be kicked off.
- Clothes with tiny buttons—they're difficult to handle.

☐ Remember that a medium size, once washed, often turns into a small.

☐ If the garment is in a package, open it before you buy to visually check the size. Labeled sizes vary and can be completely misleading.

☐ Check the care labels before you buy. If you like to wash the baby's clothes with soap flakes for softness, you may be annoyed to find that the sleeper you buy must be washed in detergent to keep the garment flame-resistant.

☐ Spray overalls with fabric protector (such as Scotchguard) so that spills will bead instead of becoming absorbed.

☐ If you always buy tops and bottoms basically in the same basic colors (blue, red, yellow, green), everything will always match everything else.

☐ When buying two-piece pajamas, buy multiple pairs of the same style so you're not always searching for the "other half." Also, this way, if one half becomes ruined, you don't have to throw out the whole pair.

☐ The kimono is useless for a fall/winter baby. Get stretch suits instead.

☐ Terry cloth stretch suits are wonderful. Baby is covered from top to toe in one garment, which enormously simplifies dressing. They also stretch and give for freedom and comfort. The stretchy quality means they fit a bit longer, too.

☐ Don't figure on buying seven stretch suits for seven days. In the beginning, seven stretch suits will last you about two days, if you're lucky.

☐ Pants with elastic waists droop with diapers, get soaked easily (they can act like a wick), hang down below fat tummies, and generally look sloppy. Buy them only for toilet-trained children. Overalls look best on diapered babies.

☐ Don't ever buy shirts that have to be tucked into pants. They never are. They often come as part of pants/vest outfit. The shirt will always be hanging out below the vest.

☐ Cotton clothes (unlike polyester or acrylic) do not hold odors from milk, spit-up, etc. when properly washed. They are also better for babies with sensitive skin.

☐ Don't bother to hem pants that are too long. They look cute with rolled-up cuffs, and you'll need the extra length as your child grows. Use suspenders if they're too big around the waist.

☐ Don't buy "next season's" clothes early. You don't really know what size your baby is going to be.

☐ Return the seasonal-type clothes you receive as gifts and get a credit. Since you don't know how big the baby will be, they might be the wrong size in the wrong season.

☐ The cloth on the outside of some styles of plastic pants acts like a wick and gets very wet. Plain plastic is better.

☐ Don't buy plastic pants with snaps. They rip off too easily after several washings.

☐ Buntings are convenient because they're simple to put on. But:

- They're hard to use with some car seats and strollers because of the crotch strap.
- They can't be used with a chest carrying device (like a Snugli).

☐ Don't buy buntings without arms. Baby is too hard to lift that way.

☐ A hat is necessary in spring and summer to shield baby's head from the sun.

☐ Babies seem to prefer hats that hug the head, like ski hats, to hats that tie under the chin. Of course, if baby insists on pulling the hat off, you'll need one that ties.

☐ A hat worn day and night might be necessary in a very cool house. A lot of body heat is lost through the head.

☐ In the winter, snowsuits or buntings with hoods eliminate the hat problem.

Shoes

☐ Ask your doctor; everyone seems to have a different theory. Some mothers we spoke with recommended a pair of sneakers as soon as baby started standing; others said they had been advised to hold off on shoes until baby was walking outdoors.

☐ *Never* let a salesperson sell you shoes that are too small or too big. In the beginning, try to buy shoes in stores that specialize in kids' shoes and which employ trained personnel.

☐ Have your baby's shoe size checked about every six weeks.

☐ Babies don't need ankle-high shoes unless your doctor specifically recommends them.

☐ Buy shoes with laces or they'll never stay on. Baby moccasins and such are adorable but totally impractical.

☐ Sandpaper the soles of new shoes to keep them from being too slippery. Or tape on some adhesive tape in a T shape (with the cross of the T near the toe).

☐ Double-knot shoelaces. Babies love to untie them and are clever at learning how.

☐ When the ends come off of shoelaces, apply clear nail polish or short pieces of Scotch tape.

☐ Keep an extra pair of shoelaces in your supply closet.

☐ You can throw sneakers into the washing machine along with the rest of the laundry (but only with similar colors). Allow laces to dangle from one hole only. Air dry to avoid shrinkage.

☐ By now, everyone must know that you can slide boots on over shoes more easily if you put a plastic bag over the shoe first.

Used Clothing and Hand-Me-Downs

☐ Scout garage or tag sales for infant clothes. You can usually get a year's worth of clothes for less than four or five new outfits would have cost. Also, since babies don't usually wear anything for very long, most used clothes look pretty new.

☐ If clothes at a tag sale are *very* clean and *very* pretty, they've probably never been worn because they're *very* impractical. Think twice before you buy them.

☐ If you are a new mother, ask another mother to come with you to tag sales. She'll help you avoid the impractical stuff.

☐ Used clothes have been child tested. They won't shrink any more, and if they've lasted long enough to be sold in good condition, they're pretty durable.

RECYCLING OLD CLOTHING

☐ Don't give up on stubborn stains before you check the stain removal section on pp. 50–53.

☐ Don't throw away infant-sized clothes. They'll make great wardrobe for the right-sized doll later on.

☐ Dye or tie-dye badly stained undershirts and T-shirts.

☐ Sew fancy appliqué or iron-on patches over worn areas on pants and tops. Patches trimmed with pinking shears stay on longest.

☐ Lengthen pants by sewing a fancy trimming or *preshrunk* grosgrain ribbon to the cuffs.

☐ You'll get an extra year's wear out of a jacket or snowsuits by sewing knitted cuffs (you can get these in dime stores or at notion counters—or cut the cuffs off discarded sweaters) to the sleeves.

☐ Remove fuzz from sweaters by "shaving" the surface lightly with a razor blade.

☐ Use Velcro strips for hemming overalls or replacing old fasteners.

☐ Consider sewing little bells to the toes of booties. Babies love them.

☐ You can make stuffed toys (which are only slightly stuffed but mostly flat) in the shapes of animals and letters of the alphabet and attach these to the front of a child's overalls with snaps. They look cute, cover stains, and are especially good when you're traveling since they "attach" to your child.

☐ Soak garments in cold water with a bit of white vinegar added to prevent colored fabrics from running.

☐ Cleaning fluid or cuticle remover, applied with a moist cloth, will remove most stains from children's shoes.

☐ Use heavy-duty #8 thread for sewing on buttons. They'll stay on much longer that way.

☐ Beeswax rubbed on thread makes it very strong and less apt to twist. You can usually find it at fabric stores.

☐ When a stretch suit is too short (but the rest still fits), cut off the feet and sew longer socks or booties to the bottoms.

☐ If you love her in those overalls, but they're too hot for summer, cut off the legs to make them into shorts.

Dressing the Baby

☐ Tuck the sleeves of an undershirt (the kind that opens in the front) into the sleeves of the stretch suit. Then you put baby's arm through his sleeve only once instead of twice.

☐ Use one-piece summer outfits with the snap bottoms as underclothes in the winter. They don't ride up, and baby's tummy stays warm.

Baby's Laundry

☐ For information on stain removal, see pp. 50–53.

☐ Keep a nylon net on a hook near the changing table. When you undress your child, put socks and booties (or anything very small) in the net. Put the tied-up net in the washer with the rest of the laundry. This way, the small stuff doesn't get jumbled up with the other clothes and is easy to find and sort. (Use the same method for keeping outgrown clothing that you want to wash once more and then store separate from the rest of the wash.)

☐ Put a cup of white vinegar in the second rinse water to get *all* the soap out of baby's laundry.

☐ Add ⅓ cup baking soda to the rinse water to make baby's laundry smell fresh.

☐ Air-dry plastic pants. Dryer heat makes them brittle.

☐ To prevent shrinkage, avoid hot water and automatic dryers unless you have one with a no-heat setting.

☐ If your baby has sensitive skin, wash clothes with soap rather than detergent and make sure they're rinsed well.

☐ Keep some laundry stain remover (like Spray 'n Wash) near the changing table, and use it on dirt and stains before you put the dirty clothes in the hamper.

☐ A good investment is a wooden clothes rack that folds out in the bathtub. Air-dried clothes don't shrink.

☐ A wet cloth dipped in baking soda will remove odors. Just dab at the fabric. This will work on most spit-up (and other) baby odors. Try to apply soon after the "accident" happens.

Your Clothes

If you buy any new clothes for yourself after the baby comes, remember:

☐ Be sure they're washable. You cannot imagine how dirty you get and how quickly you get dirty.

☐ You'll want *pockets* for the tissues and paper towels you'll be carrying around to mop up drool, spit-up, etc.

☐ Dark prints hide dirt, drool, and leaking milk.

☐ Fitted shirts you buy when you're nursing will be too big later. Stretchy sweaters are better.

☐ See the stain removal information that follows.

Stain Removal

☐ Before applying any stain remover directly on the affected spot, first experiment with it on some portion of the garment that is not visible just to make certain that the remover is safe for the fabric.

☐ Put the baby's laundry in the machine to soak overnight with detergent or a commercial presoak. In the morning wash it. This method will take care of most stains.

☐ Make sure stains are out before putting clothes in the dryer. Dryers set stains in.

☐ For stubborn stains, mix equal amounts of dishwashing liquid (like Joy) and ammonia. Store this mixture in an empty squeeze bottle and apply to spots before clothes go into the washing machine. (Do not wash with chlorine bleach when you do this.)

☐ The proper time to deal with a stain is *immediately!* The longer you wait, the more difficult it will be to remove it. Remember, once the stain is set, it can be difficult to remove completely.

☐ Use the following guide for removing common (to some of us, anyway!) stains:

BLOOD

Absorb as much of the blood as you possibly can with a paper towel and then soak in cold water. Scrub with soap or detergent and rinse with cold water. You can also try dabbing hydrogen peroxide on a fresh blood stain, but test the fabric first for color fastness first.

CANDY

Soak in warm water. If stain persists, add a few drops of white vinegar and denatured alcohol to the water. Rinse.

CHEWING GUM

Place garment in freezer. Remove from freezer when gum is brittle enough for you to crack. If traces of the stain remain, wash with soap and water.

CHOCOLATE

Sponge first with cold water and then with the following solution: 3 tablespoons borax to 3½ cups warm water.

DIAPER RASH OINTMENT

Use a commercial spot remover (like Carbona) especially made for grease stains.

EGG

Soak in a solution of 1 quart warm water, 1 tablespoon ammonia, and ½ teaspoon liquid detergent for about a half hour. Rinse.

FRUIT AND VEGETABLE JUICE

Soak in cold water and then, while spot is still wet, rub detergent into it. Rinse.

GRASS

Sponge with white vinegar or denatured alcohol. Rinse thoroughly.

MILK AND ICE CREAM

Soak in cold water and then wash with water and soap or detergent and rinse. If stain persists, sponge with safe cleaning fluid. (Be sure to test the cleaning fluid on an unexposed portion of the fabric first.)

MILK (REGURGITATED)

Wash immediately with cold water and sponge with a small amount of diluted ammonia. Rinse. If this is not possible, use a damp cloth or sponge to dab some baking soda on it, which will at least take care of the smell.

MUCUS

Soak in cold water and then rub soap into stain. Rinse.

MUD

Allow to dry and brush off. Sponge with borax solution (see CHOCOLATE, p. 51). Rinse.

PETROLEUM JELLY

Scrape off as much of the jelly as you possibly can and blot the stain with a commercial spot remover (like Carbona) made for grease stains.

URINE

Soak in cold water, wash with soap, and then, if stain has not been removed, sponge with mild ammonia solution (see EGG, p. 51). Rinse.

VOMIT

Soak in cold water and then sponge with mild ammonia solution (see EGG, p. 51). Rinse. Again, a damp cloth dipped in baking soda will take care of the odor.

4
Furniture and Accessories

Although new cribs and many other baby accessories are required by law to meet certain safety standards, it is advisable that you use common sense in all your purchases. If you're in doubt about the safety features of an item—or if something just doesn't seem "right" to you—*don't buy it*. You'll rest easier if your own safety standards have been met in addition to those of the government.

Bassinet

☐ A carriage can be used instead of a bassinet. If you put it by your bed, you can soothe a fussy baby by rocking it without even getting up.

☐ An old wicker basket, rejuvenated with a coat of bright-colored *nontoxic* paint and decorated with ribbons and lace, makes a lovely bassinet that will have other uses later on (toy storage, laundry basket, or even a wagon—add wheels and a rope for pulling it along).

☐ Drawers lined with soft blankets are ideal for tiny babies.

Just make sure the bottom is firm like a mattress, not soft like a pillow.

☐ The fancy bassinets sold in stores are beautiful, but remember that baby will outgrow the bassinet in a few short months.

Crib

☐ A new crib is a good investment, because it will have been built according to Consumer Products Safety Commission's standards, set in 1973. Secondhand cribs might be dangerous. Check any old crib against the new standards, which are:

- The distance between the crib slats must be no more than 2⅜ inches. This is not only to keep baby's head from getting stuck; more importantly, this very small opening insures that baby's wiggly body stays inside the crib.
- The inside must measure 27¼ inches by 51⅝ inches to fit a standard crib mattress. The Consumer Product Safety Commission gives this guideline: If you can fit more than two of your fingers between the sides of the crib and the mattress, then the mattress is too small.
- The paint must be nontoxic, the hardware safe, and all surfaces smooth.
- The movable side must be at least 26 inches higher than the mattress support at its lowest position to keep baby from climbing out easily.
- Some crib headboard and footboard designs may allow an infant's head to become caught in the openings between the finial (top of the bedpost) and the robe rail (horizontal piece along the top of the crib), or in other openings in the headboard structure (see illustration).

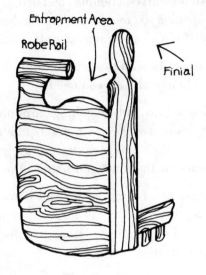

Entrapment Area

Robe Rail

Finial

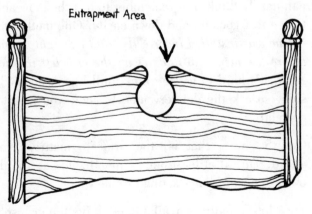

Entrapment Area

Crib Safety

This may lead to strangulation. Look for a crib design either without the curved openings and bedposts, or one where the opening is too large for the head to get caught. Many finials can be unscrewed and discarded.

☐ Be aware that the cribs with two movable sides cost more. One movable side is really all you need.

☐ If you're buying a crib with matching furniture, choose designs and styles that will remain practical after you've removed the crib. (Pink and blue designs for babies may look inappropriate by the time your baby is two.)

☐ The crib mattress can be moved up and down. Use the highest level when your baby is tiny and remember to adjust it downward as he grows. (Many parents forget!) It will really save your back.

☐ When the crib arrives, you are usually so dazzled that you can hardly think, but remember to test the moveable side to see if it goes up and down easily. One mother told us, *"Mine was installed incorrectly, and I caught the problem before the men who had set up the crib left the house."* Also, it's hard to get the kick/pull knack of moving the side, so ask the delivery men to show you how to do it correctly.

☐ Get the best—that is, the firmest—mattress you can afford. Turn it at least once a month, just as you do your own, to ensure long-lasting firmness.

☐ The "best" mattress available often fits the crib so tightly that it becomes extremely difficult to change the sheets. Test the mattress inside the crib you buy to see if it's easy to maneuver. (Note: It should fit snugly for safety, but it does not have to be tight.)

☐ A crib is a piece of furniture you use and look at a *lot*. It helps if you really like it. A few mothers reported that they were glad to have gotten the slightly more expensive—and attractive—one.

☐ Consider getting spring casters for the crib. This way, you can rock the crib.

☐ Stretchy cotton knit fitted sheets are much easier to put on crib mattresses than the percale kind. They adapt well to slightly different-sized mattresses, too.

☐ Bumper pads for the crib are essential. They protect the baby's head as he flops around, minimize drafts, and keep baby's toys from falling out. Safety standards dictate that they tie or snap onto the crib in at least six different places.

☐ Make sure the bumper pads are of good quality. Since you have to take them off the crib every time you change it, check to see if the fasteners are sturdy. A curious child playing in a crib can demolish them. More importantly, loose or broken fasteners are a health hazard.

☐ Bumper pads covered with cloth will last much longer than most plastic-covered ones.

☐ Protect the crib mattress with a plastic covering if it is not already covered with a waterproof material.

☐ Use flannel rubberized mattress covers. Use small ones over the large one in strategic places (baby's head, baby's bottom), so if the smaller pad gets soiled you don't have to change everything. If you can't buy the small-size cover, buy a large one and cut it up. By the way, save these covers; they'll come in handy if your child has bedwetting problems (they're very common) when he switches to a regular bed.

☐ Babies do not need pillows. In fact, they're a hazard. Do all you can to resist the fancy ones you'll see in stores.

Changing Table

☐ Even the youngest baby can roll off a changing table. Don't *ever* leave the baby unattended even for a second.

☐ The kind of changing table that folds in half is practical when you have a walking baby who likes to pull everything out. You can just close it up!

☐ A wicker changing table is very useful. It holds an endless number of baby items for the first two years and makes an attractive plant holder later on.

☐ A large shelf (3′ × 5′), waist high, with a covered foam pad, works fine. Make sure it is sturdy enough to support baby's weight.

☐ Slip a pillowcase over the changing-table pad. That way you can keep it clean by changing it as often as necessary.

☐ Use the crib as a changing table. If you have to leave the baby, just pull the side up.

☐ Change baby on the floor; then there is no danger of rolling off.

☐ Putting the changing table in a corner and a dresser at an angle next to it gives you plenty of room and easy access to changing necessities and storage.

☐ A carriage pad or mattress on top of a dresser works well. For a safety belt, take an old belt, cut it in half, and staple the two ends to the top of the dresser.

☐ If you're not neat, a dresser used as a changing table hides the mess better than those open storage-type changing tables. (You can throw everything into the drawers.)

☐ Put hooks at the end of the changing table for baby's wet bath towels, security blankets, clothing, etc. Make imaginative use of the wide variety of decorative acrylic and plastic hooks and shelves available on the market. These are great for holding washcloths, towels, clothing, etc. A bath specialty shop is an excellent source of such finds. Hooks that attach to the wall by means of small suction cups are especially useful here.

☐ Hang a paper-towel rack near the changing table. You'll need it.

☐ Whatever you use as a changing table, consider putting a shelf above it. The shelf can hold diapers, powder, distracting toys, etc. You can easily get what you need, but it's out of the reach of curious toddlers. Under the shelf you can rig a mirror, hang a nice picture, or hang a mobile for baby's entertainment.

☐ Make sure any shelves hung over a place where baby might sit, sleep, or play are very secure. Use appropriate hardware for hanging such a shelf if your walls are made of plaster or wallboard.

Carriage and Stroller

☐ Don't invest in an expensive carriage if your baby is born during cold months and won't be able to go out much anyway. Try to borrow one instead, or buy one second-hand.

☐ The carriage with the removable sleeping basket can also be used as a portable crib when traveling or as a place for baby to nap.

☐ Don't get a carriage pillow. Babies don't need them, and they're hazardous.

☐ Umbrella strollers almost unanimously win over all others.

☐ An umbrella stroller can be hung from a large hook in a closet or on a garage wall.

☐ Make sure that the carriage or stroller you have has brakes.

☐ Try to buy a stroller with front wheels that swivel. They're *much* easier around turns. If you have a stroller that doesn't have swiveling front wheels, find out whether it can be converted.

☐ Tie a few toys to the side of the carriage or stroller so that the baby can retrieve them as they're tossed out. Make sure the string you use isn't long enough to wrap around the baby's neck or hands.

☐ If the handlebar on your carriage or stroller is too low and you find yourself hunching over to push it, find out if your local infant-furniture store carries the kind of handlebar that can be attached to the existing one to make it higher.

High Chair

☐ Metal high chairs clean better than wooden ones and are easier to get into a car.

☐ The portable "high chair" (made out of cloth—you put it on the baby and tie it to a chair) is very practical for restaurants or visiting friends who don't own high chairs.

☐ Get a high chair with a completely detachable tray so you can remove it later on and let the baby sit at the table with everyone else. Also, it's much easier to keep clean.

☐ Feeding tables are cute but impractical. Babies don't usually like to stay in them very long, they're harder to clean, and you have to bend over to feed the baby.

☐ Put a piece of foam rubber in the seat of the high chair to keep baby from slipping.

☐ The base of the high chair should be wider than the seat. Beware of any chair that looks like it may tip over.

Car Seat

See pp. 151–153.

Automatic Swing

See pp. 137–138.

Other Accessories

☐ Toy chests look nice, but their lids can fall and injure your child. Try various sizes of wicker or plastic baskets for toys. You can toss the stuff in quickly and baby can empty them safely. Shelves are nice for large toys.

☐ A mesh portable crib is much easier to handle than a wooden one. If you're going to move it a lot, buy the mesh.

☐ A portable crib can double as a playpen in a pinch, but it doesn't give a growing baby much room.

☐ If you get a rocking chair, make sure it has arms; otherwise you have nothing to rest the weight of the baby on.

☐ When buying a rocking chair for the nursery, remember that wood is easier to clean than upholstery when you have spills of milk or formula, or when baby spits up.

☐ Be sure your rocking chair is well-balanced so you won't tip over if you're holding twenty-five pounds up at shoulder height.

☐ Consider having a bed, cot, or couch in baby's room for yourself. One mother pointed out, *"Many nights I would just conk out there rather than trudging back to my own bed after nursing. And it's helpful to have when the baby is sick and you want to sleep in her room."*

☐ A playpen is great *if* you can get the baby to be happy there for any length of time. Some babies refuse to stay in it.

☐ Let an older child climb into a playpen with the baby only if the older child is gentle enough to be trusted.

☐ Get an infant seat. Your baby will be all the more portable, and it gives him a better view of the world. It can be used for everything from feeding to napping. (Note: It cannot be used as a car seat. See pp. 151–152). One mother attested to the usefulness of an infant seat as follows: *"Casey was a winter baby and it was usually too cold and windy to take him out during those first months. The professional nurse we'd hired had a great solution. She would dress him warmly, bunting and all, and put him in his infant seat, which she placed in his carriage. She'd let him sit in front of an opened window, and he'd be delighted to watch the activity outside and get fresh air as well. I'm convinced it made Casey eat and sleep better."*

☐ A safe infant seat has a wide base so it can't tip over.

☐ Once again, please make sure what you buy for your baby is safe. Check your library for books and magazines with product safety information (ask the reference librarian for help). There are many products which are actually hazardous. If in doubt about a product, call the Consumer Product Safety Commission's hotline:

> (800) 638-8326 (Continental U.S.)
> (800) 492-8363 (Maryland residents only)
> (800) 638-8333 (Alaska, Hawaii, Puerto Rico, Virgin Islands)

The commission will send you free fact sheets on baby products upon request.

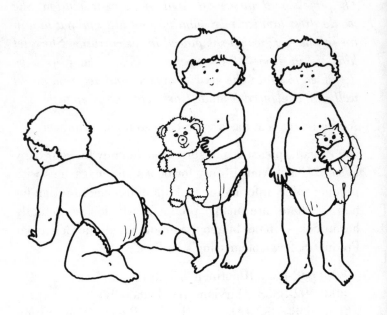

5

Diapers and Diapering

Cleaning, Wiping, Powdering

☐ The pop-up, premoistened baby wipes are impossible, because you have to hold the container with one hand and pull with the other, which leaves no hand for baby. And more often than not they rip.

☐ Warm those disposable wipes between your hands before you clean baby.

☐ Soak a roll of toilet paper in a shallow bowl containing about 6 ounces of baby oil. Wait until it's absorbed, and presto—you've got baby wipes that destick anything. The toilet paper should be fairly strong; don't use the soft, fluffy kind.

☐ Or soak a stack of soft napkins the same way. These can be stored in plastic sandwich containers.

☐ The BM comes off much better if baby's bottom has been previously coated with petroleum jelly.

☐ To clean BM's, put petroleum jelly on a tissue and spread it on. Then take a clean tissue and wipe it off.

☐ Put the oil or ointment on with one finger only and wipe the residue off on the diaper before you pin or tape it.

☐ If you use oil to wipe baby clean during a changing, put the oil in some kind of bottle with a spout (like an old shampoo or hand-cream bottle) so it's easy to dispense.

☐ Warm the baby oil by placing the bottle in a pan of warm water. Baby will appreciate it. Wouldn't you?

☐ If you prefer to clean baby's bottom with washcloths, it helps to have them color coded, so you'll know which ones to use for what. For instance, the cloths with the blue trim are always used for baby's bottom, and never get confused with the yellow ones used for the bath.

☐ When baby's really messy, just stick his bottom under the faucet to rinse him off.

☐ Keep warm water in a thermos bottle in the nursery for those middle-of-the-night diaper changes.

☐ If you use powder, shake it carefully into your hand first, then put it on baby. Shaking powder directly on baby puts a lot of it in the air, and it's not good for baby to breathe.

☐ Check the ingredients of commerical baby products, especially powders. Often they are made of simple, inexpensive ingredients, like cornstarch, that you can buy for much less at the supermarket.

☐ Put cornstarch in a small powdered-sugar shaker (the kind with holes at the top) to keep handy for diaper rash problems. Add some baby powder to the cornstarch for scent. (That's all the commercial preparations contain!)

Diapering Made Easy

☐ If you live in a two-storey house, keep the baby's supplies (diapers, powder, etc.) on *both* floors. It will save a lot of running.

☐ For a snug fit, tape the side closest to you first. Then roll the baby toward you to tighten and fasten the other side.

☐ Disposable diapers with elastic legs are wonderful for newborns because their bowel movements are so runny. (Don't use them when the baby has diaper rash, though. The rash needs fresh air to heal, and these diapers let very little air in.)

☐ To make disposable diapers snug around the legs so the BM won't fall out, try this: Take tucks in the legs of the diaper and seal them with masking tape. This is easiest when baby is on her back with her legs in the air. Put the tucks right under her fanny.

☐ If the disposables seem too large and have gaps around the thighs, just tuck them up and in.

☐ Masking tape will hold disposable diapers together if the sticky tabs break. Keep a roll near the changing table.

☐ One mother made the following observation: *"Pampers seem to be made for boys. I found they worked better for my daughter when I put them on backwards."*

☐ When diapering a boy, point his penis down so his tummy won't get wet when he urinates.

☐ Discount toy stores usually sell disposable diapers cheaper by the carton.

☐ Buying cheaper brands of disposable is not always a money-saving move. Check and compare thickness and absorbency.

☐ If you are interested in economizing, use cloth diapers for at-home days and save disposables for going out.

☐ Keep a special toy or household item (keys, plastic cups, spoons) on a shelf or in a drawer near the changing table. Give it to your baby when she fusses on the changing table, but only then. It will retain its special distraction value for a long time.

☐ At changing time, it helps if you have a routine you *always* follow and talk about. ("Now take the pins out. Pins are sharp. Ouch!") Babies will learn to anticipate and laugh. A special game that you always play helps, too. (See Chapter 10 for ideas.)

☐ Always talk and sing to your baby as you change him. This is as stimulating as touching or seeing you, and baby loves it.

☐ Instruct baby-sitters—or anyone else who might feel uneasy about diapering—to do it on the floor—if there are no pets around. Remember, babies can't fall *off* the floor.

☐ Drop a room deodorizer in the diaper pail.

☐ Regardless of how the instructions on the package read, don't flush disposable diapers down the toilet.

☐ Dunk soiled diapers in the toilet as you flush.

☐ To soak diapers, place them in a covered pail of water to which you have added one teaspoon of borax. Launder when you're ready.

Diaper Pins

☐ Keep your diaper pins stuck in a bar of soap (out of baby's reach). The soap makes them glide through the diaper very easily.

☐ It's hard to stick safety pins in if they're not sharp. Invest in new ones whenever yours seem dull; it's safer and easier for you and the baby.

Diapering Defiance

At around eight or nine months, many babies who have previously endured diapering without a whimper suddenly become whirlwinds of defiance, merely because you have put them on their backs to be changed. This is normal behavior, but it's frustrating for the adult who has to live with it. These suggestions might make it easier:

☐ Diaper teddy bear first.

☐ Give baby something to make him feel useful ("Chris, please hold this diaper for Mommy").

☐ Change in front of the TV.

☐ Take some masking tape and stick it on her fingers or wrist. As baby gets more adept at pulling it off, you can make the "tape tangles" more elaborate.

☐ Diaper baby as he's standing.

☐ Begin a question-and-answer routine that will catch her attention and distract her. For instance, this one works very well:

"What does the cow say?"
"Moo-o-o-o!"
"What does the duck say?"
And so on.
Add funny facial expressions and she'll be changed before she knows it.

☐ Talk to baby rapidly and seriously. Tell him *anything* that's on your mind. He might not understand, but he'll be engrossed in trying to figure it out.

Extra Overnight Protection

My son woke up soaked every morning until I heard how another mother had double-diapered with disposables. I'd just never thought to do it. Here are some ways to keep baby drier:

☐ Put on one disposable. Rip the plastic open in the front and back. Then put another diaper on top (use the kind with elastic legs if there's a runny BM problem.)

☐ Detach diaper at top and slip another one inside (both pieces of plastic are now on the outside).

☐ Cut a cheap diaper in half, pull off tabs, perforate the plastic, and use it inside a better diaper.

☐ Add a sanitary pad to the diaper.

☐ If there's no diaper rash problem and baby still wakes up wet, use rubber pants over the two diapers.

Diaper Rash

☐ Put diaper rash ointment on *before* a rash occurs. Once a day is a good preventative.

- [ ] Use soap and water and clean thoroughly. Air baby's bottom, then put ointment on to protect the irritated skin from urine or BM.

- [ ] Cornstarch works well to soothe skin.

- [ ] For sun in the winter, put bare-bottomed baby in front of a sunny window.

- [ ] Fasten disposable diapers loosely so air can get in.

- [ ] If baby is wearing disposable diapers, change to another brand or cloth.

- [ ] If baby is wearing cloth diapers, change to disposables.

- [ ] Change diaper frequently (for example, immediately after BM or urination).

- [ ] Watch the juices baby drinks. Cut down on amount and change kind.

- [ ] It's worth the effort to do extra changing during the night.

- [ ] If baby tends to get diaper rash, don't double-diaper or use plastic pants, because you are keeping his clothes dry at the expense of wet skin.

- [ ] For prickly heat, dab with a mild solution of baking soda and water (about a tablespoon to a bowl of water). *But be careful*. The solution makes baby slippery.

- [ ] If a rash hasn't healed in two days after your own treatment, call your doctor about it.

PERSONAL EXPERIENCES

Two mothers came to the following conclusions about diaper rash:

"For seven months my son had a bad fungal rash that my doctor's prescribed medicines couldn't cure, even though I used them faithfully. Then we went to the beach. I took the baby's diapers off for two days, let him run around in the sun, and the rash healed. It's messy if the baby's not toilet trained, but it's worth it!"

"I let Rachel run around bare-bottomed for half a day upon my doctor's advice to clear up a rash. Watching her romp through the house so happily made me realize that she was hardly aware of her own body, since she spent all her time dressed. She loved seeing herself in a mirror naked. After that, I tried to let her run around without clothing each day for just a few minutes before I dressed her for the night. When she was very small, I could place her on a waterproof pad for this special playtime. I must admit that it got to be messy as Rachel became more mobile, but it certainly seemed worth the trouble."

Diaper Service

☐ *"Disposables were a disaster because my child's bowels were so loose,"* said one mother. *"I changed to cloth diapers and a diaper service and was much happier. For one thing, I didn't have to lug all those boxes home from the store."*

☐ Prefolded diapers are more absorbent and easier to manage.

☐ If you have two children in diapers, diaper service is a lot cheaper than disposables. Check it out.

☐ Don't be afraid to deduct money for poor service.

A Final Word

Years ago there was a movement toward toilet-training children at a very early age, sometimes as early as one year or eighteen months. But current studies, and the mothers we talked with, indicate that there is no such thing as toilet training—that children do it when they're ready (when their sphincter muscles are properly developed, for instance), and that forcing a child to approach the stage prematurely will result in problems later on.

If friends and family pressure you and call to tell you about the fourteen-month-old down the street who is toilet trained and then ask you whether your baby is trained yet, just tell them, "No. Is it a problem?"

6
Food and Feeding

Newborns

☐ It's important to keep your newborn awake during feedings, especially if she has any special feeding problem due to prematurity, cleft palate, etc. If you are having trouble, see the techniques suggested for premature babies on page pp. 33–34.

☐ If baby can't suck very well, use a pacifier between feedings.

Breast Feeding

I heard these tips over and over:

☐ Have patience. Lots of it. Be persistent—it gets easier every day.

☐ If you're having trouble or need support, get in touch immediately with the La Leche League. The league is dedicated to helping mothers breast-feed successfully. Don't hesitate to give the league volunteer a call. She can often solve the problem on the spot. Many mothers don't even call the La Leche League, because they are afraid of being pressured by people who are overly enthusiastic about breast feeding. Don't prejudge the league and its members. Try going to their meetings a few times. If you don't like them, then you don't have to go back. And you don't have to do everything they recommend to have an enjoyable breast-feeding experience. To locate the group in your area:

- Look in the White Pages of the phone book under "La Leche League."
- Ask your ob/gyn or pediatrician.
- Ask any hospital.
- Ask any Lamaze instructor.
- Check with the people you know who have breast-fed.
- For a free information packet on breast-feeding and baby care and the location of your local La Leche group, call or write:

  La Leche League International
  9616 Minneapolis Avenue
  Franklin Park, Illinois 60131.
  (312) 445-7730

☐ Quite often a newborn can't grasp your very full nipple, and breast-feeding becomes frustrating. Squeeze the areola from the top and bottom (so it becomes more like the shape of the baby's mouth) and ease it in. If you have trouble, ask a nursery nurse to help you.

☐ Put a pillow on your lap and rest the baby on it.

☐ If you're nervous, have a glass of wine. It not only relaxes you, but it eases the pain as the baby latches on in the beginning.

☐ Right from the beginning, get into the habit of drinking juice or milk as you're nursing to replace the liquid that's going out.

☐ Put your finger into the corner of your baby's mouth when you want to take him off the breast. This breaks the suction.

☐ Music can help you and the baby relax.

☐ It's hard to get the hang of hand-expressing milk. The methods shown in books don't always work. It's best if you can ask someone to show you how.

☐ You have to *learn* to nurse lying down. It doesn't come naturally. Experiment and find a comfortable position for you. Pillows behind your back help. As your baby grows and becomes less limp, it gets easier.

☐ Stick a bobby pin on the strap of your bra to show which breast you started nursing baby on. At the next nursing, start with the other breast and move the pin.

☐ Some babies prefer one breast and refuse the other. Just be persistent in offering the other breast and eventually the baby will take it.

☐ Don't worry if baby's mouth doesn't cover the whole areola as all the books say it must. One mother reported: *"I always tried to cram more in, but the baby knew what to take, and maybe I have extra large areolas. Anyway, he nursed and grew just fine. I think the books are trying to make sure you don't let the baby just grab the nipple alone."*

☐ Keep a pitcher of ice water or juice handy and really try to drink a lot.

☐ Even if you plan to breast-feed exclusively, try a bottle of water occasionally right from the beginning to get baby used to it, so that if a bottle becomes a must during an emergency, it'll be that much easier on the baby. You might want to express your own milk for the bottle.

☐ Make a "necklace" out of spools, clothespins, ribbons, etc., to wear when you're nursing. If you've ever worn a regular necklace when nursing, you know how babies love to touch it.

☐ What *you* eat may have an effect on your baby. Some nursing babies seem especially sensitive to cow's milk, chocolate and caffeine (found in coffee, tea, cola drinks, various medications). Try herbal teas for a morning drink. Carob is a good substitute for chocolate.

☐ Before taking any medication, check with your doctor to make sure it's safe to take while breast-feeding.

IN THE BEGINNING

☐ For a change of pace, straddle the baby on your lap, facing you.

☐ For some reason, many people ask how long you're going to nurse. One mother handled it this way: *"I always gave an arbitrary date (like nine months or a year) to end the conversation. I had no intention of stopping till the baby and I were ready, but I didn't want to discuss that with insensitive people."*

☐ Breast feeding can be lonely and boring at times. Since most people (including husbands) assume you want to be alone, you must tell them you need their company.

☐ Do accept all the help (with housework, cooking, etc.) you can get. If you are exhausted from trying to do too much, you will not be able to produce enough milk for your baby.

SORE NIPPLES

☐ If you have sore nipples, try soothing them with;

- A & D Ointment
- Cocoa butter
- Lanolin
- Commercial breast cream
- Baby vitamin drops (let dry—they stain)
- Breast shields

☐ *Never* use soap on them. Don't even let shampoo fall on them.

☐ Air nipples after each feeding at least ten minutes.

☐ Take a hot shower or apply hot compresses and hand-express some milk if your nipples are hard and sore.

☐ Acetaminophen (like Tylenol) will help relieve the pain.

☐ As baby takes hold, do your Lamaze panting breathing.

☐ Even if nipples are cracked and bleeding, continue nursing. Try a breast shield.

☐ Remember, the pain will eventually go way.

LEAKING MILK

☐ Put the baby's waterproof crib pad on your *own* bed.

☐ Press firmly on nipple with the heel of your hand.

☐ Spread a waterproof crib pad on your lap while nursing so you won't get soaked.

☐ Cut a sanitary napkin in half and stuff in your bra.

☐ Cut up a disposable diaper and wear it in your bra plastic side out.

☐ Wear black sweaters or dark print tops to hide stains.

MASTITIS

If you feel feverish, and your breasts feel tender and are mottled with red, you've probably got mastitis. Call your doctor at once. In the meantime:

☐ Let the baby nurse as long and as frequently as possible on the infected breast.

☐ Apply hot compresses. Wash cloths or small towels work best. Hot showers feel wonderful.

☐ Check to make sure your nipples are not clogged with dried milk.

☐ To avoid recurring infections, the minute you feel a lump start to develop, use the hot compresses and get the baby to empty the breast.

Bottle Feeding

☐ Boil the nipples with toothpicks in the holes to keep them open.

☐ Enlarge (or make more) holes in rubber nipples with a sewing needle heated with a lighted match.

☐ Pour boiling water over the feeding equipment to sterilize it. This way you eliminate the danger of putting everything in to boil, forgetting about it, and then burning the nipples.

☐ Save money: Don't buy a bottle sterilizer. A large pot will do just as well.

☐ Bottles will get sterilized if you wash them on the lower rack in your dishwasher.

☐ Soaking clean bottles and nipples for a few minutes in a baking soda and water solution takes away any lingering odors. Rinse well.

☐ If your baby constantly seems to have diarrhea, you may be evaporating too much water when you sterilize, thereby concentrating the formula. Try sterilizing bottles on the bottom rack of the dishwasher and using boiled water to mix with the formula. It's much easier, and it may put an end to your baby's diarrhea.

☐ Too many bottles are hard to keep track of, and you always find one here and there with sour milk. Once a baby is on solid food, it's a good idea to keep only one or two bottles on hand.

☐ To keep baby bottles from flying all over the dishwasher, tie them up in a drawstring net bag before you stick them on the prongs.

☐ Put a bottle in a colorful sock to make the bottle less slippery and easier for the baby to hold.

☐ Formula is much more expensive in individual 8-ounce cans, but they're awfully convenient when traveling.

☐ *Always* check the expiration date on formula cans.

☐ Use bottle straws, so that baby will be drinking no matter what position the bottle is in.

☐ Ear problems can develop if you let a baby drink a bottle while she's flat on her back.

☐ Those plastic bottles that come in the shapes of clowns and bears are cute, but they're *much* harder to scrub clean. Avoid them; they'll make weaning more difficult anyway!

☐ When nipples start to deteriorate, get rid of them! Always keep a supply of new ones on hand.

☐ You don't *have* to warm bottles.

Burping

☐ Remember that babies don't *always* burp after every meal.

☐ Try putting baby face down on your lap (covered with a towel) and giving her back a gentle massage.

☐ When breast-feeding, burp the baby between breasts to make sure she'll be able to get all she needs from the next breast.

☐ Try gently sitting baby upright for burping.

☐ A bubble can collect as much as an hour after feeding—even if you burped the baby after the feeding.

Weaning

☐ Follow your child's lead. Pick a time when he's showing independence and capitalize on it.

☐ Substitute something for the nursing. For instance, anticipate when he'll be hungry and offer food (say Cheerios) before crankiness starts. Soon Cheerios will represent relief from hunger instead of nursing.

☐ If you're trying to wean your baby but whole milk makes her colicky, try powdered milk for a while, and *very* gradually, little by little, add whole milk.

☐ Remember that a child will drink about one-half as much from a cup as she will from a bottle. Bottles and nursing satisfy sucking needs as well as hunger.

THREE MOTHERS' METHODS

"For two weeks I gave my child an empty cup to play with in the high chair. Gradually I added a little bit of liquid (first juice, then milk). But I never took away the bottle. Now at meals I offer milk in a cup and a bottle and she's choosing a cup more and more." (Try this method when weaning from the breast and you may avoid bottles altogether.)

"Watch for signs of lagging interest in the bottle and act quickly to teach the use of the cup. These signs include drinking only a few ounces and then playing with the bottle and nipple. My first two children learned to drink from a cup at five or six months, and by a year they were

completely weaned. But with the third, I was too busy and missed the optimum time to make the switch. At eleven months he's still clinging fiercely to the bottle."

"At five months, I dropped one breast-feeding a week so baby and I could get used to weaning gradually. The first dropped was the lunch feeding. I offered her a bottle of breast milk, but she wouldn't take it. Nor would she take formula or regular milk. The second week I dropped the mid-afternoon feeding. But she still wouldn't take a bottle of milk, although she'd happily drink juice from a bottle. I was getting worried that she wasn't getting enough milk. I kept offering the bottle only to have it refused, and I was about to give up by the third week when, suddenly, she took it. Things went smoothly from then on."

Solid Food

☐ Nurse until baby grabs for food. You'll certainly know she's ready then.

☐ Introduce new foods slowly—one at a time for a week—so that if baby has an allergic reaction you'll know what caused it.

☐ During mealtime, you can name and spell out what baby is eating, talk about the color, size, and texture, and compare it to his other foods.

☐ Demitasse spoons are just the right size for baby. So are small hors d'oeuvre forks. (Make sure they're not sharp.) Some babies find forks easier to use.

☐ Put a spoon in each of the baby's hands and feed him yourself with a third spoon. He won't be able to resist imitating what you're doing and will soon learn to feed himself.

☐ Use an egg poacher for heating a variety of foods at the same time.

☐ Save those baby food jars. They're great for storing nails and hardware, buttons and sewing items, and lots of other "little" things.

☐ Baby food jars are not heat resistant.

MAKING BABY FOOD

☐ Be sure to grind it up for the baby *before* you've added any seasonings.

☐ To get the right consistency, use meat or vegetable broth for extra vitamins instead of plain water for thinning. Use wheat germ or dry cereal for thickening.

☐ Fill up ice cube trays with your own pureed leftovers and cover with freezer wrap. One or two cubes will make a meal.

☐ If you're freezing your own baby food in ice cube trays, store the cubes in plastic containers or bags marked with the name of food and date.

☐ Freeze some food in small covered containers. You can pull them out in a hurry if you've got to rush somewhere close to mealtime, and they'll be defrosted by the time you get where you're going.

☐ *"If you serve baby your own fresh-cooked vegetables at an early age, he will probably not put up a fuss about them later,"* a mother said. *"My children have always enjoyed fresh broccoli, cauliflower, and other vegetables because they were introduced to these flavors early."*

FINGER FOOD

☐ Put small amounts of food in each part of a cupcake tin, and let baby choose the finger food of his choice. Aluminum trays with divided compartments or similarly designed paper plates are also convenient.

☐ Be careful with teething biscuits, cookies, or any dry food. Baby can gum them, bite off a large chunk and choke. While these foods are fine for children to eat, just be sure you're watching them and can take immediate action if necessary. For instance, don't give dry foods to baby in the car.

☐ Avoid beets as finger food. They're recommended often but make the worst stains.

☐ This is not meant to be a complete list of all possible finger foods, but it may give you some new ideas:

- Apples (As with most fruit, slice and peel for easy handling, although some babies like them whole.)
- Baby lamb chops (for older babies with teeth)
- Bagels
- Bananas (Coat banana slices with dry baby cereal to make them less slippery.)
- Bean curd
- Berries
- Breadsticks

- Broccoli
- Carrots (cooked, but firm)
- Cauliflower
- Cheerios (the most universally popular)
- Cheese
- Chicken drumsticks (for older babies)
- Dried fruit
- Fish cakes or fish sticks
- French fried potatoes
- Gefilte fish
- Graham crackers
- Grapes (Cut in half for children who might swallow them whole. Freeze, too, for a surprise treat— especially when baby is teething.)
- Green beans
- Hot dogs
- Italian bread
- Melon slices
- Noodles (in a form easy to hold, like wheels)
- Orange slices
- Pears
- Pickles
- Pineapple
- Popsicles (yogurt or frozen fruit juice)
- Raisins
- Rice cakes
- Shredded wheat (bite size)
- Toast
- Tuna fish chunks
- Zucchini

WHEN BABY WON'T EAT

Forcing a child to eat is never desirable. Babies will eat when they are hungry, and if they don't, there is usually a good reason. But there are times when you want to introduce a new food, or you *know* the baby is hungry but just too cranky to eat. These techniques may be persuasive:

☐ Put a Cheerio on top of the food in the spoon.

☐ Try to distract her with funny faces to change her mood. Sing funny songs.

☐ If a new food is rejected, mix a little of it with a favorite food such as fruit. Gradually reduce the fruit.

☐ Sometimes he'll take food from a blunt butter knife rather than a spoon.

☐ Change the consistency or texture of the food. A mother told me, *"My baby wasn't a good eater until I stopped feeding him pureed mush and gave him lumpier and coarser food."*

☐ Don't always feed baby in the high chair. Put her in the middle of a plastic tablecloth and have a picnic for a change.

☐ If she can handle an egg (both yolk and white), put one in a blender with her milk or juice and give it to her in her bottle.

☐ When baby is temporarily distracted, food will stay warm if placed over a pan of hot water.

☐ Try using colorful, unbreakable plates made just for kids.

☐ Ignore the baby and go about your business in the kitchen. Quite often he'll start feeding himself.

☐ Don't worry if baby gets "hung up" on just two or three foods. She'll get interested in new ones when she's ready.

MINIMIZING THE MESS

☐ Tie washcloths, bottles, and toys to the high chair to avoid having constantly to pick up thrown objects.

☐ The heavy plastic bibs are easy to clean, and the scoop at the bottom catches spilled food.

☐ Take advantage of warm weather when teaching your baby to feed himself. Dress him in as little as possible and have mealtimes outside where messes won't matter.

☐ A cowboy bandanna makes a cute bib.

☐ Keep your floor clean by putting a washable tablecloth (or newspapers, or whatever suits your fancy) under the high chair.

☐ After she's finished eating, put some water in a shallow plastic bowl on the baby's tray and she'll be delighted to clean her own hands.

☐ Let baby practice eating messy foods or drinking from a cup in the bathtub.

☐ Dispense with the plate altogether in the beginning. Just put food on the high chair tray. That way, baby can't throw the plate.

☐ Put a lazy Susan or plastic turntable in your refrigerator to keep all those jars organized and accessible.

☐ A chunk of charcoal (not to mention an open box of baking soda) will absorb refrigerator odors.

☐ Make a poncho bib by cutting a hole (for baby's head) in the center of an old plastic tablecloth. Trim as needed. This poncho will also come in handy for haircuts, finger painting, etc.

☐ Attach a hook or towel rack to the back of the high chair so you'll always have a place for your cleanup cloth.

☐ Take the high chair outdoors occasionally and hose it down with the garden hose.

EATING OUT

Don't be afraid to try it. Remember, the tiniest babies often adapt the best, because they like to sleep so much.

☐ Make sure the restaurant is geared to families.

☐ Go out *only* with supportive, understanding people.

☐ Well-fed infants will often sleep happily through your dinner in a chest carrier, car seat, or infant seat.

☐ In general, babies under a year do better if they're not hungry when taken out to eat. They're usually happy with the distraction. After a year they tend to want to eat with you, so bring them somewhat hungry.

☐ Always have familiar food with you for a fussy baby. Cheerios were always a part of our restaurant meals.

☐ Egg coddlers keep favorite foods warm (or chilled) and seem more suitable to nice surroundings than plastic containers.

☐ Take a belt with you to the restaurant so you can strap the baby in the high chair. Quite often the belts have been broken or lost.

☐ Portable cloth "high chairs," available in children's accessory stores, turn any chair into a safe place for baby.

☐ Carry your own booster seat into restaurants, in case there aren't any or the ones there are in bad condition.

☐ The car seat can be used in restaurants.

☐ Take the umbrella stroller in with you, and if baby's cranky, she can be pushed back and forth for a while.

☐ Carry a restless child around the restaurant with you before the food comes—or let him walk if he can.

☐ Ice cubes almost invariably entertain a fussy baby. So do straws and crackers.

☐ Take your baby out for Chinese food! Babies love the filling in egg rolls and the wontons without the soup. A sparerib should keep an older baby occupied for a good length of time.

☐ Babies love to tear paper napkins. It's a great diversion. Just make sure you clean up the mess before you go.

☐ If the waiter or waitress has been especially understanding about baby's needs, show your appreciation by tipping accordingly.

7

Sleeping

Sleep Patterns

Sleep patterns are very individual; don't let your mother, grandmother, or some authority tell you differently. Some parents drive themselves mad at first trying to make the baby follow a "normal" four-hour eat-and-sleep schedule, since they hear so often that "infants sleep all the time"—not so, in many cases. You may find comfort in the following variations:

"It seemed as if my baby never slept, and life was chaos until at three months, I started keeping a diary of the times he was awake and asleep. After about five days I could see a pattern: He liked being awake for about two hours and asleep for about one. From then on, if he started to get cranky after two hours, I knew he needed sleep and put him to bed. It was a great relief to stop worrying if I was doing the right thing. Even if he fussed about being put down, he usually fell asleep after a few minutes. This pattern lasted until he was about six months old."

"Both my children were practically round-the-clock sleepers until they were about four months old. But I did

*wake them up about every three and a half hours during
the day so they'd be sure to get enough to eat and adapt
to some sort of schedule. Also I wanted to make sure they
learned to wake up during the day, not at night."*

*"My child had day and night reversed after coming home
from the hospital. We couldn't do anything about it until
I had lots of relatives over one day. She was so excited
that she stayed up all day, and that night she slept. That
was it—she made the change herself."*

*"At one month my baby started going to sleep for the
night at five P.M. He'd wake up at one A.M. to nurse and
at five A.M. for the day. Nothing I could do changed this.
The pattern changed itself at six months. If you have a
similar problem, be patient—this, too, will pass."*

Getting Baby to Sleep

☐ Swaddle and walk. (After two months, walking can
become a habit that is hard to break.)

☐ Put baby in bed, and if he fusses, go *"Sh-h-h-h!"* This
will surprise him, and if you're lucky, he'll stop. Walk
quickly out of the room.

☐ Be sure to warm the bed, bassinet, or cradle with a
heating pad. Take the pad *out* and check the temperature
of the bed before you put baby in.

☐ Hold baby firmly against your chest, sit on the edge of
your bed, and bounce hard for a few minutes. A father
told us that he tried this because in the womb, the baby
was always quiet when the mother was active. He figured

that all that bouncing calmed him down. This worked, off and on, for almost three years.

☐ Get babies outside as much as possible. Fresh air seems to tire them out and make them sleepy.

☐ While nursing, make sure to cut out your intake of caffeine (coffee, tea, cola drinks, some over-the-counter cold medications) if your baby is having trouble sleeping. Some babies are really sensitive to it.

☐ A fan circulating the air in the baby's room not only cools the baby down in the summer, but the humming noise really helps some babies sleep *and* blocks out the noise from older brothers and sisters.

☐ If the air in baby's room is dry, get a humidifier. The moist air might keep baby sleeping more comfortably, and the humming sound is comforting.

☐ If your child finds a certain noise relaxing and sleep-inducing (one baby liked the hair dryer), make a tape of it and play it every time he goes to sleep. Once he is asleep, you can gradually turn down the sound before you turn it off.

☐ Your child may sleep better when she hears voices and general household noises. It makes some babies feel less lonely.

☐ Quiet, lulling music might relax your child.

☐ A cranky baby will almost always fall asleep during a car ride.

☐ Putting springs on the legs of the crib can be a lifesaver. That way you can rock the baby to sleep.

☐ A gentle back rub helps.

☐ *"My husband got our baby to sleep by putting her head* firmly *against his shoulder, walking her a bit, and telling her it was time to sleep,"* one mother reported.

☐ A bath relaxes some babies before bedtime. Others are very stimulated by the playing. Experiment.

☐ Watch for your child's "sleep signs." One mother told me, *"Soon after I brought my son home from the hospital, I noticed that he'd always rub his nose on the sheet before he went to sleep. Then at certain times during the day, he'd rub his nose on my shoulder, and it finally dawned on me that he was signaling for sleep."* Another mother said, *"You might say that David generally ran on a speed of 7. When he wound up to 10, he was really frantic and ready for sleep."* Rubbing of eyes and yawns are obvious sleep signs. More subtle signs are sudden crankiness and irritability. You will soon be able to interpret your own child's signals.

Bedtime

☐ If your baby doesn't want to go to sleep until 2:00 A.M. or so, try putting her in fifteen minutes earlier every night. This slow, gradual process works.

☐ Always change your baby's clothes before you put him to bed for the night, even if you're putting him in the same kind of stretch suit he's worn all day. He'll get the signal eventually that *now* it's time for bed and the "long sleep."

☐ If your baby needs to nurse to fall asleep at night and you'd like to break this habit, try these ideas:

- Keep her up so late that she'll fall asleep whether she nurses or not.
- Get her father (or grandmother, sitter—anyone but you) to put her to bed for a few nights while you *leave* the house.
- Put her in bed awake. She'll cry and fuss, but be firm.
- See information on changing baby's habits, pp. 210–211.

☐ Bedtime rituals are very helpful if your baby needs quieting before bed. They have to be done in the same order each night to be effective. Some suggestions are:

- Sing songs (lullabies, etc.).
- Say good night to stuffed animals or other objects in room.
- Read the book *Goodnight Moon*—a real favorite!
- Pull the shades and/or curtains with baby (have him "help" if possible).
- Look at a short picture book (older children will enjoy *short* stories).
- Briefly discuss baby's day.
- Wine up a crib mobile.
- Rock in a rocking chair.
- Make a big deal out of turning off the light (older children like to turn the light off themselves).

☐ Children may eventually tire of a certain routine. They show it by becoming restless or cranky. Just develop a new routine, incorporating something more appropriate to the child's age and taste (i.e., reading storybooks rather than singing songs).

☐ As your child grows older, don't incorporate anything you don't really enjoy into a routine. Toddlers can become exceptionally inflexible and demand *exactly* the same thing every night.

Waking at Night

☐ An intercom is essential if your bedroom is quite far away from baby's room and you worry about hearing him at night. Intercoms are not very expensive, nor do they need special installation. Some plug into any electrical outlet; others are battery-operated.

☐ If you keep baby in a cradle or carriage by your bed, her fussiness at night can often be soothed by rocking the cradle, and you won't even have to get out of bed. Tie a short string to the side of the cradle facing you and you'll be able to rock easily.

☐ Instead of changing a soaking-wet but *very* hungry, crying baby, wrap him in a warm quilt, feed, then change.

☐ If the sheet is wet, don't change it in the middle of the night. Put down a flannel-covered rubber pad and/or quilt for baby to sleep on.

☐ Ready-to-feed bottles are worth the expense for nighttime feedings. By the time you've warmed up a bottle, baby is awake, and it takes that much longer to get him to sleep again.

☐ If you're nursing, leave a large glass of juice next to the chair you nurse in at night so it will be all ready for you.

☐ Watch television if you're dozing from boredom and exhaustion. Or turn on some soft music.

☐ Don't make a big production out of night feedings. Keep lights low, movement to a minimum, and baby won't think it's time to be awake.

☐ Glow-in-the-dark stars that you stick on the ceiling may keep baby amused during the night. Be sure to point them out.

☐ Use overhead lights during the day, but only a bedside light at night. The softer light will let baby know it's still nighttime.

☐ If you install a dimmer switch in baby's bedroom, it's very easy to adjust the light to what you need.

☐ Try not to count the hours of sleep you're *not* getting. Five hours a night sounds worse than it really is.

☐ At around nine months, teething pain may wake baby up screaming. Distract him by walking around the house, giving him milk and sometimes baby aspirin. (See TEETHING, pp. 212–213.) Check with your doctor.

☐ Cold temperatures can wake a baby up. If your child doesn't keep a blanket on, make her a poncho from a warm blanket by cutting a hold for her head in the center, or use a blanket sleeper.

☐ If he does not tend to get rashes, then put on a double diaper, rubber pants, a terry stretch suit, and then a heavy blanket sleeper, so that he will not wake because of cold and wetness.

BREAKING THE HABIT: SOME PERSONAL EXPERIENCES AND PRACTICAL ADVICE

☐ *"I wanted my child to sleep through the night when he was about nine months old. I was exhausted, and he didn't really seem very hungry when I went in. My pediatrician suggested this routine: Go in when he cries (to show him I was there and I cared) but tell him that I wasn't going to pick him up and that he should go back to sleep. Then leave the room and don't go back. Knowing this would be difficult, I gave it a week. I figured I could stand anything for a week if it meant I'd eventually get an uninterrupted night's sleep. And if the baby wasn't ready to sleep through, then I'd go back to getting him up and feeding him. The first night was awful. He must have cried for at least an hour. And I was a nervous wreck. The next night he cried for about a half hour and the next night he didn't wake up at all! There was some backsliding a couple of times. When he was sick, I would naturally comfort him when he woke up at night. But as he got better, I could see he was getting into the wake-up habit again, so I had to let him cry."*

☐ If the baby cries while you're teaching him to sleep through the night, don't lie in the dark and suffer. Turn on the TV, read a good book, play card games—it will be less painful for you.

☐ If you're a nursing mother, ask your husband to go and comfort the baby. One mother said, *"I think the smell of milk from me drove the baby wild—nothing but nursing would do. Her father had much less trouble getting her back to sleep."*

☐ *"At five months, when my baby started waking up, I checked to see if he was wet, gave him one ounce of water in a bottle, put him back down. He cried, but didn't wake up again."*

☐ *"At around eight months, our second child would wake up every night at about two A.M. and stay awake for two or three hours no matter what we did. She was happy as long as we were holding or playing with her, but would cry*

*incessantly if we put her back in the crib. We finally solved
the problem by eliminating her naps. Apparently she just
didn't need that much sleep."*

☐ *"My child had woken up every night for eighteen months.
Then my husband and I went away for four days and left
her with a baby-sitter. When we returned, she was cured."*

Naps

☐ Be confident and positive you're doing the right thing
when you put baby in for a nap, and chances are she'll
believe you.

☐ If your child falls asleep while nursing, but wakes up
when you put him in the crib, try putting him on a mat on
the floor instead of in the crib.

☐ Clear the crib of toys. The absence of distraction settles
babies down quickly.

☐ *"Naps were not a problem if I made sure the baby got some
physical activity and exercise in the morning and afternoon,"* one mother said. Fresh air helps, too. Try to go on
outings before nap time.

☐ With older children running around, your baby may find
it hard to settle down. A fairly long, familiar prenap
routine (pulling down shades together, singing songs)
works best.

☐ Before the baby's born, establish a "quiet time" with your
older children in the morning and/or the afternoon so that
they can get used to it before the baby arrives.

☐ Leave a sign on your front and/or back door: Don't
Disturb—Baby Sleeping.

☐ Take the telephone off the hook during naps. If the buzzing disturbs you, dial *0* and stick a pencil in the dial so it can't return. Or just unplug the phone.

☐ Babies get used to household noises very quickly; when they want to sleep, they'll sleep through practically anything. So don't feel you always have to tiptoe around.

☐ Let baby take daytime naps in a playpen or carriage. Then she'll know that when she's placed in the crib it's nighttime.

☐ One mother related the following experience: *"Up until my child was about one year old, I had been waiting for him to get obviously tired before putting him down for a nap in the afternoon (he'd already dropped the morning one). But it began to make planning anything impossible, so I announced one day at lunch (as if it were the most normal thing in the world) that he'd be going in for a nap right after lunch. 'No, no, Mommy!' he cried. But in he went, and although there was fussing and crying, I kept up the routine, and in a couple of weeks, he completely accepted the after-lunch nap and went right to sleep."*

☐ If your baby is content to lie awake and just *rest* during nap time, let her.

The Early Riser

☐ Set a clock radio to go on and entertain him.

☐ Keep the room as dark as possible (try room-darkening shades or curtains). Tiptoe in as if it were the middle of the night and whisper, "Go back to sleep. It's not time to get up." Then leave. If your bedroom is close enough to the nursery, don't go in, just call out gently.

☐ Put *favorite* toys in the crib before you go to bed for baby to play with in the morning, or put toys in the crib that baby is not allowed to play with at any other time. Playing cards fascinate many babies. You'll find them scattered all over the place in the morning.

☐ Share the burden. You take the 5:00-to-6:30 shift and let your spouse take over from there.

☐ Keep a cot in baby's room to rest and doze on while baby plays with a special toy she gets *only* in the morning.

☐ If baby wakes up for a bottle of milk, try giving him water. It may take a few days to get this to work, but eventually he might not even wake up for the water. If somebody gave you warm milk and lots of love at 5:00 A.M., wouldn't you wake up for it, too?

☐ See the information changing baby's habits, pp. 210–211.

Bedding

☐ Some babies sleep better with soft quilts over their hard mattresses. Be sure quilts are tucked in well or under the sheet so baby doesn't get tangled up in them.

☐ Never put a pillow in baby's bed. She doesn't need it, and with a newborn there's a chance of suffocation.

☐ Small stuffed animals or cloth dolls in the crib give baby something soft to snuggle up to.

☐ Receiving blankets don't really function well as blankets—at least not for a winter baby. They're okay for swaddling, though.

☐ Sew four no-longer-used receiving blankets together to make a larger summer-weight blanket.

8

Crying

All babies cry. Some cry more than others, and we all must try to remember even as they're screaming in our eardrums that at first it's just about the only way they have to communicate. Often there's an obvious reason for the crying—hunger, fatigue, teething, etc.—but many times you simply have no idea why they're crying.

Obviously, the first approach to take with a wailing child is to try to figure out what's wrong and then correct it. If you've checked all the possible causes of the crying and not found the reason for it, you've got a problem. Here are some possible solutions:

Soothing Infants (One to Three Months)

These tips have worked for children in this age range, but many of them are also effective for older babies. You never know when a certain technique is going to work for your baby, so if something does not work at two months, try again at four months.

☐ Keep the baby in motion in a cradle, a rocking chair, a wind-up swing, a carriage, your older child's wagon, or,

107

of course, your arms. Put springs on the legs of the crib and rock the baby there.

☐ Give baby something to suck. Try a pacifier or your fingers. If your baby won't take a pacifier, keep offering it. (Just remember that you may be starting her on a habit that may be difficult to break later on. See THE PACIFIER: GIVING IT UP, p. 211.) Some infants who refuse it at one month will take it at three months. If baby still spits it out, try one of these:

 • Just as baby is being lulled to sleep by the motion of the car on a nice long drive, slip the pacifier in her mouth. Quite often, this will do the trick.

 • Dip the pacifier in sugar water or fruit juice before giving to baby. (Traditionally, pacifiers have been dipped in honey. If you do this, make *sure* the honey has been boiled (pasteurized) or do it yourself. Most honey you buy is "raw" and may contain substances harmful to babies under six months.

☐ Lay the baby on his stomach across your knees and gently move him from side to side. Rubbing his back or the back of his head sometimes helps too.

☐ Play the record *Lullaby from the Womb,* a recording of sounds baby heard in the womb. You have to use it right from the beginning, though, so baby will recognize these sounds.

☐ Play any kind of music that you think will soothe you and the baby.

☐ Swaddle the baby. Here's how: Put him on a small, square blanket so that one corner is above his head. Bring the opposite corner up over his feet to his chest. Fold in each of the side corners one at a time. Make sure baby is snugly wrapped with arms in. (See illustration, p. 110.)

☐ Put baby in a chest carrier while you walk, do housework, etc.

☐ Take her for a ride in the car.

☐ Try holding baby upside down by the ankles *for a few seconds only*. It's weird but it works, even for babies a month old. It probably just startles him so that he forgets why he's crying. Don't do it just after baby's been fed, though.

☐ Dance with baby. Try different kinds of music—lullabies, rock 'n' roll, ragtime—and hum along. Some infants show a definite preference for certain rhythms.

☐ When baby is overtired and overstimulated, hug her very tightly.

☐ See if the sound of your hair dryer or vacuum cleaner will soothe her. One mother reported that the sound of her hair dryer quieted her baby so effectively that she taped it on a cassette and used it often—with great success!

☐ Carry the baby with his fanny on your hip and your hand around his stomach, even if he just dangles there. A pediatric nurse suggested this, and reports that most babies quiet down in this position. (See illustration, p. 111.)

☐ Bathe the baby, or bathe *with* the baby if you're tense and irritable, too. It really works to relax both of you, and it's fun.

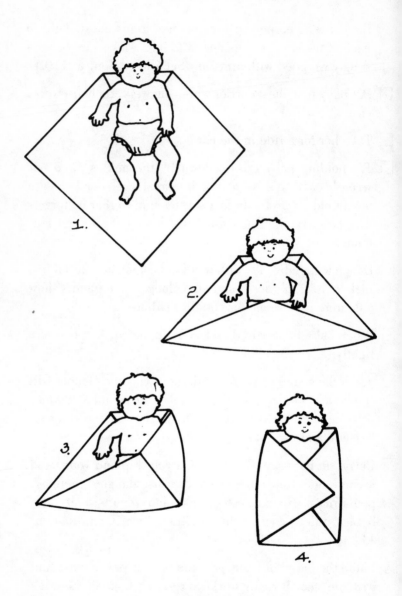

How to Swaddle a Baby

The Hip Carry

☐ Call a friend who has that certain knack with children and ask her to take over for a while. Sometimes a baby who continues to cry is reacting to your frustration with his crying.

☐ If the crying won't stop, the baby might be sick. Do call your doctor for advice on this. One mother told me, *"My child has only cried twice for hours on end and I eventually took him to the emergency room. Both times he had ear infections.*

☐ If you're confident that baby is not wet, dirty, stuck with a diaper pin, sick, etc., then occasionally try letting baby work out of the crying spell by himself. Too much fussing over baby can lengthen a crying spell.

☐ If you've tried everything, just put the baby to bed and get as far away from the noise as possible. Wash dishes or play some music to drown out the noise. The baby might just fall asleep.

☐ If nothing else seems to be wrong with your newborn but she won't stop crying, the umbilical cord may be bothering her. If it hasn't fallen off after a week at home, talk to your doctor about getting it off.

COLIC AND STOMACH PROBLEMS

☐ Try the "colic carry": Put baby stomach down over your arm with the head in the crook of your elbow. Make sure the head is higher than the stomach so baby can burp easily.

☐ Burp baby as frequently as possible, especially during nursing or bottle feeding. It's a bore, but it can really prevent gas buildup.

☐ Don't stop breast-feeding.

☐ Poke more holes in rubber nipples (four or five) with a hot sewing needle. This makes the formula flow faster and reduces air intake.

☐ Feed baby in a semisitting position.

☐ Ask your doctor about soy formula without corn syrup or corn solids. It makes a big difference for many babies.

☐ Hold baby as tight as you can without hurting him and rub his neck.

☐ Put her in a bed with a *warm* hot water bottle under her tummy. Make sure it is warm, not hot. You could also warm a spot on baby's bed with a heating pad. But *don't ever put a baby on one of these pads*. Electricity and wet babies don't mix!

☐ Try giving her a bottle of lukewarm fennel, comfrey, or camomile tea.

☐ Put baby on his stomach over your knees and let him suck your knuckle or a pacifier.

☐ If you're nursing and baby seems to have colic, it may be something *you're* eating that baby is allergic to. Cow's milk often causes problems. Try not drinking it (or eating any milk products) for a while and see what happens.

☐ Here's one mother's experience with colic:

"My son had a spell of crying each evening when he was two or three months old. My doctor assured me that there was no disease that only comes on in the evening, so we knew we were dealing with colic. We found that the more

we fussed with him, the longer the crying spell would last—sometimes up to five hours. Then I worked out this routine: When he started crying I swaddled him, let him cry for twenty minutes, then picked him up to comfort him briefly, and put him down again. This would usually shorten the crying spell to a half hour or forty-five minutes. I felt very cruel at first leaving him to cry, but finally I realized I was doing all of us a favor by getting it over with as quickly as possible."

Soothing Older Babies (Four Months and Up)

These suggestions might also work for younger babies, but they seem more effective for older ones. Try these distraction techniques when you've run out of your own ideas:

☐ Take the baby's clothes off.

☐ Change him, even if he doesn't need to be changed.

☐ Try laughing, even if you don't feel like it.

☐ Sing peppy songs, songs with funny noises ("Popeye, the Sailor Man"), songs with high and low notes ("Ol' Man River," "The Erie Canal"). Really let go, screw up your face, ham it up.

☐ Change his location, even if just to another room. Outside is best.

☐ Give him a new toy, although it doesn't really have to be new. Put certain toys away for a few months and bring them out during crying emergencies. Or have a toy exchange with your friends. Other babies' toys are always fun, and when your own come back, they'll seem like new.

☐ Push him in his stroller, even if you're stuck indoors.

☐ If baby always seems to get cranky or fussy at a certain time of day, plan a specific activity he likes for that time, like a long walk outside in the chest carrier.

☐ If a stranger makes your baby cry, tell the person to ignore the baby.

☐ Take the baby to a mirror, point at her reflection, and ask, "Who's that crying baby?"

☐ If you child is crying because he has bumped into something and is more startled than hurt, try scolding the offending object by saying, "Bad table leg!" (or whatever it was). At around seven months, most babies find this routine hilarious.

☐ Make light of all those tumbles and spills your walking child will have. If she's not really hurt, the tears will vanish quickly. Too much solicitous attention may convince her that she really did hurt herself.

Living with the Crying

☐ Use earplugs or earmuffs. Cut down the noise and you won't go crazy. If you're calmer, baby might be, too.

☐ Get someone to stay with the baby and get away for a short while. You'll have more patience when you return.

☐ If there's nobody there to help, put baby in a safe place, like the crib, get away from the noise, and
  - Take a shower (it drowns out the noise).
  - Jump rope, run in place, exercise away your anxiety.
  - Set the timer for a certain amount of time, say five or ten minutes. Do yoga or something supremely relaxing. *Don't go back* until the timer rings.

☐ Try not to feel guilty! Many mothers admitted that they took the crying personally, thinking that the crying was *directed* at them. In less tense moments it was easy to understand that such an idea was just silly.

Some Observations About Crying

☐ *"My children got really cranky when I was tired and was trying to do too much. The only thing that worked was to stop what I was doing and give them about twenty minutes or so of undivided attention."*

☐ *"There were some days when my baby seemed to fuss and cry all day. Perhaps he was teething or maybe he was sick—it's so frustrating not to know. Anyway, he and I would both go crazy on those days because I would try to keep things on schedule and he would make everything impossible, from feeding to changing.*

"One day he started up again and I just decided that something must be wrong with him, because he generally was fun to be with. So I changed my attitude. I made up my mind to cater to his needs exclusively. If he wanted to nurse all day, fine. If he wanted to be held, fine. If he didn't want to eat, fine. Well, it was just amazing. It didn't take long before he was quiet and content. And I felt so

relaxed because he wasn't ruining my day—my day was his day.

   "Then I was scared that he'd be spoiled and always expect this kind of exclusive attention. But, surprisingly enough, he was perfectly happy to go back to his normal routine in a day or two."

9

Bathing

Making It Easier

☐ *Never* leave baby unattended in the bathtub—not even for a second!

☐ As in all other matters, act with confidence. If baby knows you're unsure of what you're doing, it will make him uneasy as well. Try to maintain cheer at all times—it really does help!

☐ Take the phone off the hook during bath time, so you won't be tempted to run off and leave the baby unattended if there's a call.

☐ It is a myth that *all* children love their bath. If you sense your child doesn't like it, be *super*gentle with her right from the beginning, and don't do it too often, and maybe you'll avoid real trauma. Don't shampoo each time you bathe.

☐ If you keep their bottoms clean, babies don't need a bath each day.

☐ Hasn't everyone heard this one? Always test the baby's bathwater with your elbow, because your hand is not sensitive enough to the water's temperature.

☐ Your finger cleans in and around all those double chins much better than a washcloth. Be sure to get the skin between the creases clean; otherwise, sores develop.

☐ For boy babies: Be sure to pull the foreskin back so you can wash his penis thoroughly. Lint and dirt tend to collect here and can cause problems.

☐ If your baby is very heavy, or you have a bad back, it's much easier to bathe her in a sink than in the tub. Line the sink first with a towel to avoid slips.

☐ A foam rubber square (with a scooped-out place for baby's body) works well in baby's tub. He doesn't slip and your hands are free. You can buy them almost anywhere.

☐ An inflatable tub is useful until babies can sit up; then they like to be in more water. It can be used later on for outdoor water play.

☐ Line an infant seat with a towel and put it in the bathtub. With the baby strapped inside, your hands are free, and she's safe.

☐ Blowing bubbles in the bath is fun.

☐ Let the water trickle from the tap for baby's amusement. Make sure the water isn't hot.

☐ Taking a bath *with* your baby is really fun and relaxing for you, too.

☐ Turn the hot water temperature down (to below 130 degrees Fahrenheit or 55 degrees Centigrade) for the whole house when the baby arrives. That way, if she ever accidentally hits the hot water faucet, she won't get instantly scalded.

☐ After you fill baby's bathtub, turn off the hot water first, so if there are any drips, they'll be cold ones.

☐ At some point your baby will grab the washcloth you're using and hang on for dear life. Avoid struggles. Always have two or three washcloths on hand.

☐ Make gloves or mittens out of old towels (just use a rough tracing of your own hand for a pattern) to use as washcloths. They give you a better grip on baby, and they're entertaining if you decorate them as puppets.

☐ If you no longer need your receiving blankets, cut them up into small squares and use them as baby washcloths.

☐ Cut interesting shapes out of colored sponges. They make great bath toys.

☐ You don't need to clean inside an infant's ears. Just wipe the outside of the ear with a washcloth. Cotton swabs are completely unnecessary and potentially dangerous. Never put *anything* in a baby's ear.

☐ Bathe baby right along with an older child. They'll both love it.

☐ Don't get rid of your baby bathtub. It has many uses, such as a small wading pool or a winter "sandbox," which can be filled with cornmeal or uncooked oatmeal flakes.

☐ Wear a vinyl apron while bathing the baby. And no matter *where* you do the bathing, a bath mat is essential for soaking up all that splashed water. Just remember to pick it up off the floor when you're done; toddlers can skid on them.

☐ Keep a net bag or baby's bath toys near the bathtub. Hang the bag to drip dry when the bath is over. Throw the bag into the dishwasher once in a while to get the toys clean.

☐ If you wind up bathing the baby in the kitchen sink, be sure to keep your supplies (towels, shampoo, washcloths) there, so you're not constantly lugging them from nursery to kitchen.

☐ When bathing baby in the kitchen sink, be sure to swing the faucet out of the way so baby's head doesn't get bumped.

☐ Remove baby from bathtub before letting the water out. Most babies have fears of disappearing down the drain along with everything else!

☐ Try bathing an especially fussy baby in the "frog" position. Place him on all fours in the tub and use one hand to support his tummy while you wash him with the other hand. Obviously, his head should be kept well above water at all times.

☐ Save time: Take the baby into the shower with you. Hold tight!

☐ Don't worry about baby urinating in the tub; urine is sterile!

Here's a rhyme for baby's bath that teaches body parts:

> Gonna wash the little tummy
> And wash the little toes.
> Gonna wash the little knees

And wash the little nose.
Gonna wash the little hands
And wash the little hair,
And *(baby's name)*'s gonna be clean
Everywhere!

Gonna wash the little elbows
And wash the little eyes.
Gonna wash the little thumbs
And wash the little thighs.
Gonna wash the little fingers
And wash the little face,
And *(name)*'s gonna be clean
Everyplace!

Bathing Problems

Many parents reported that their babies suddenly objected to their baths at around three or four months of age. Here are some suggestions for coping:

☐ Try sponge bathing for a while.

☐ Bathe baby on your lap.

☐ If he seems afraid of the big bathtub, put his baby bathtub (or a laundry basket—the kind with lots of holes it it) in the bathtub and bathe him in that for a while.

☐ Try bathing her in a bucket. Hold her in a standing or sitting position. Some children just like to be upright.

☐ If you have trouble getting your baby *out* of the tub, let *her* pull the plug so she knows when bath time is over.

FOR SENSITIVE SKIN OR A RASH:

☐ Use water only. They don't really need soap.

☐ Try a non-alkaline soap (with a neutral pH). Ask your doctor to recommend some good brands.

☐ Try cleansing baby with non-perfumed oil on a pad instead of bathing. Such products are available commercially.

Massage

After the bath a massage is soothing. Baby will enjoy it, and you'll learn a lot about his body as well. One mother we spoke with told us that her mother had always massaged her children as infants, and at various times she had discovered a lump on one child's neck and a double hernia in another before the problems were even visible. Here's one way to give a massage:

☐ Use equal amounts of baby oil and lotion and warm the mixture in your hands before applying. Put the baby on his back and use a slow circular motion, starting with his chest and abdomen, then move up to his shoulders. Lift each arm individually and slowly massage the upper arm, forearm, wrist; then do his legs; turn him over and do his back.

☐ If you're worried about the baby getting chilled, massage in the kitchen with the oven on for extra warmth.

☐ Oil seems to make baby warmer, so use it in the winter. (Note: Some infants get rashes from oil or lotion.)

☐ If you're using oil or lotion, heat it in a pan of warm water while you're bathing the baby. That way it will be nice and warm when you're ready to apply it.

☐ Don't worry if baby fusses at first. She might need a week to get used to the new routine.

Baby's Shampoo

At some point many babies begin to dislike shampoos. Try these techniques.

☐ Shampoo at the kitchen sink and use the kitchen spray. Spread a towel and put baby on her back on the counter top next to the sink, or hold baby like a football with her face up and her head over the sink. Of course this works at any sink, but if you have a spray it's really easy.

☐ Sit on the edge of the tub (with your feet in the tub) and put the child face up on your lap. You can wash and rinse his hair quite easily.

☐ If the child is too big for a counter top or your lap, a low table or stool next to the bath works fine. Use a hand towel for a neck pad.

☐ Talk animatedly to your baby while you shampoo. Your facial expressions might distract him.

☐ Put a stripe of petroleum jelly across the baby's forehead to deflect drips of water.

☐ Try the head-wetting game: First pour water over arms, tummy, back, etc. By the time you get to her head, her fear may have subsided.

☐ From one mother: *"From the time my baby was three months old, I splashed the water a lot and sprinkled his face and head (later, he did it back to me). This game has made shampooing and rinsing quite easy."*

☐ Have your child hold a mirror while you lather her hair. She'll love to watch and forget about complaining.

☐ Bring a doll into the bathtub and let your child wash the doll's hair while you wash his.

☐ One mother's technique: *"Playing with the shower massage distracts the baby so that I can wash her hair. We all get very wet, but at least the hair gets washed."*

☐ Babies who shower with their parents are less fearful about getting water on their heads or in their eyes.

☐ Use a baby hair conditioner after shampooing your baby's hair to avoid all those tears during combing.

☐ If your child really hates it when you shampoo his hair, ask someone else to do it for a while. *"My son got so he only cried when I washed his hair"*, said one mother.

☐ Use a squirt bottle for dispensing shampoo. This way it's easier to control the amount of shampoo used.

☐ Remember that you don't *have* to shampoo each time you bathe the baby. Unless there are special problems, two times a week is sufficient.

Cradle Cap

Cradle cap,—that flaky, dirty-looking stuff on the baby's scalp—is not harmful, but most parents don't like the way it looks and want to get rid of it. Here are some ideas:

☐ Apply cornstarch three times daily until it dries up. Then gently rub baby oil on the scalp a couple of times during the day, and use a soft baby brush to remove scales.

☐ Apply baby oil or petroleum jelly to baby's head before bed to give the oil a chance to loosen scales. In the morning, shampoo gently but firmly and rinse carefully. You should be able to brush out most scales.

☐ Prell shampoo (undiluted) and a soft washcloth will take care of it. Note: Keep shampoo out of baby's eyes. (See BABY'S SHAMPOO, p. 125.)

☐ A cortisone cream (which must be prescribed by your doctor) is sometimes the only thing that works.

☐ Shampoo baby with an adult dandruff shampoo (like Head and Shoulders). But be sure to keep suds out of baby's eyes. (See BABY'S SHAMPOO, p. 125.)

10

Games, Toys, and Amusements

General Observations

☐ Don't inundate baby with lots and lots of toys. She will better appreciate each one if she has only a few at a time. Rotate toys as soon as the baby becomes bored with the selection. If you have friends with small children, suggest trading toys and books. By the time your own child's things get back, they'll be interesting once more.

☐ Avoid toys that are too advanced for your baby. He'll only be frustrated by them, and he won't be able to enjoy them when he does learn to use them correctly.

☐ Always use your own good sense when it comes to judging the safety of toys. In addition, consider the following points:
- Don't let a child play with anything smaller than her fist.
- Avoid sharp corners, points and edges.
- Avoid any toy with small parts that can break off and be swallowed.
- Make sure surfaces are painted with nontoxic, lead-free paint.

- Avoid toys that are not easily washable.
- Avoid anything breakable.
- Make sure stuffed toys can't easily be torn and stuffing removed.
- Cloth toys should be flame resistant. Be sure to follow their washing instructions; the wrong washing procedure will reduce the flame-retardant properties.
- Strings should not be longer than twelve inches. (Always be on the lookout for anything that can wrap around a baby's neck.)
- Beware of old rattles that might be badly constructed. There are now safety standards for these toys.

Amusements

When you run out of your own ideas, try these:

☐ Babies love to try to dig crinkly paper out of a closed hand.

☐ When baby pokes your nose, say "Honk, honk!"—she'll love it! But warn relatives and baby-sitters—she'll be poking them and expecting honks!

☐ Fake sneezes are most amusing.

☐ Even babies as young as four or five months love simple rhymes you can make up. Just include their names and repeat familiar words.

☐ Bubbles will occupy babies for a long time. You can buy the first bottle of bubble liquid in order to get the blower stick. Then just refill with soapy water made with dish detergent.

☐ Babies love to play with necklaces—especially when you're wearing them. Make a necklace of string and large beads, and let baby grab to her heart's delight.

☐ A scarf game is fun at around six months. Drape a scarf around your neck, hold one end, and put the other in baby's hand. If he pulls, move toward him. He's learning that his action creates a reaction. Then gently move away and he'll see the scarf slip through his fingers.

☐ Sit across from baby, hold his hands, and say "Give me a happy face" and make a huge grin. Then say "Give me a sad face" and pretend to cry. Do this for all the emotions you can think of—anger, disappointment, hurt, being silly, etc. Then, when you do each one again, ask baby to do it, too. After a week or so, baby will try to mimic your faces.

☐ Squirt shaving cream on a washable surface and let baby finger paint. (Use whipped cream or chocolate pudding if she insists on putting fingers in her mouth.)

☐ Empty egg cartons can be used for holding paint colors; just throw them away when playtime is over.

☐ Babies love knee games and finger games. The repetition of simple words mesmerizes them, while the surprise endings delight them. The books listed on p. 140 offer great selections, many of which you'll probably remember from your own childhood. But, if the books aren't handy and your memory fails you, don't despair. Make up your own rhymes and games. Keep them simple and sing them with love. Your baby will get the message.

☐ For a baby under three months, hang a toy out of reach and let it swing back and forth.

☐ For a baby between four and ten months: Put her in a high chair and let her play with a few ice cubes.

☐ Show home movies—especially if your baby is in them.

☐ Babies are fascinated by small animals such as birds and gerbils. They also like to watch fish swimming. Consider introducing one of these into your baby's life. But don't ever leave the baby alone in the room with a pet.

☐ Teach textures, colors and shapes to your child by helping him paste a variety of objects onto a colored piece of paper. Collecting the materials will be half the fun. Choose from the following list, or choose whatever you can find around the house.
  • Straws
  • Pictures of familiar objects in magazines
  • Pictures from greeting cards
  • Gold and silver stars
  • An adhesive bandage
  • Sand, salt or sugar (dropped on glue)
  • Uncooked macaroni
  • Pieces of fabric
  • Leaves and twigs
  • Pieces of ribbon
  • Junk mail enclosures!

☐ Hang mirrors or mirrored tiles at baby's eye level in places where she is likely to see them often. Babies *adore* mirrors!

☐ Unusual and fascinating are music boxes with dancing figurines and pendulum cuckoo clocks.

☐ Get some children's records from the library and play them often. Baby might not pay any attention to them for a long time, but suddenly he'll start recognizing the songs. So don't give up if he doesn't tune in to them right away.

☐ Set up a tent (if you have one) in your backyard and spend an afternoon crawling in and out of it.

☐ Nothing entertains a baby more than older children. If you don't have any on hand, encourage visits of neighborhood children by planning special treats for them: a barbecue lunch, homemade cookies, or a trip to the ice cream parlor. Their parents will appreciate it. (Perhaps they'll even return the favor!)

☐ Consider teaching your baby to swim. Experts say that infants have a natural ability for it. Locate a local "Y" program in your area. The weekly classes will be of great amusement for you and your baby.

Homemade Toys

☐ A long sock with buttons (or adhesive tape) for eyes makes a wonderful puppet, especially when you push the toe inside to form a "throat." Babies love to see blocks and other toys disappear inside the "throat."

☐ A plastic hanger with small colorful objects hanging from it is the simplest mobile to make. Change the hanging objects often.

☐ Take pictures of your child's friends and glue the prints onto a piece of very stiff cardboard. Then cover the whole thing with clear, pressure-sensitive paper. Babies also enjoy pictures of themselves, of their parents, and of animals.

☐ Make a family bus: Cover a milk container with construction paper and paste on contrasting-color paper for windows. Then take pictures of family members (or use those old photographs that have been cluttering your drawers) cut them up, and paste the heads in the windows. Baby can be the driver!

☐ Give a baby short pieces of Scotch tape to play with. Unsticking the pieces will keep him occupied for a good length of time. This is an especially effective diversion to use if you must be on the phone for a while.

☐ Hang a beach ball, or a balloon on a string, on a stroller or playpen at the right height so baby can push it back and forth. Make sure the string isn't long enough to entangle the baby.

☐ Make a shape box from a disposable diaper box. Just paint it and cut holes in the top to match the shapes of some household objects, like a circle for a napkin ring or a square for a block. If you don't want to get that fancy, just a hole to drop things through works fine.

☐ A fun "flash card" game for toddlers can easily be made. Glue pictures of familiar household objects on stiff paper or cardboard. Cut these pictures from magazines or draw them yourself.

☐ Fill your old baby bathtub with cornmeal or uncooked oatmeal flakes for an indoor winter "sandbox." Water play is fun, too.

☐ Make the simplest kind of dolls (even cardboard cutouts) to represent each member of the family. Don't forget pets.

☐ Make a "zoo" for all those stuffed animals. Stick colored tape on the wall to form the bars. Staple small pieces of Velcro in between the bars at random for the animals. Then sew other pieces of Velcro on the animals or on ribbons around their necks.

☐ Homemade play dough is often easier to clean up than the commercial kind, and it smells better. Here is one of the best of the many versions:

> 1 cup flour
> ½ cup salt
> 2 tablespoons oil
> 2 teaspoons cream of tartar
> 1 cup water
> a few drops of food coloring

Put all ingredients in a pot, heat, and stir till thick. Cool and knead. Store in a sealed plastic bag or other airtight container.

☐ The following household objects have always amused small children:

- Plastic containers
- Cardboard rolls from paper towels or toilet paper
- Napkin rings
- Decks of cards
- Paper napkins (they love to tear them!)
- A plastic squirt bottle filled with water
- Colored shower-curtain rings hooked together in a chain.

Store-Bought Toys

☐ Some rattles are really too narrow to fit comfortably in a baby's hand. Check this before you buy.

☐ Babies love inflatable toys that are big but light.

☐ Although some children never play with or enjoy stuffed animals, keep three or four small ones in the crib. Put them at either end and she'll probably snuggle up against them in her sleep.

☐ A dog's ball with a bell inside is more interesting than any other ball.

☐ The plastic pop-up toys that feature pop-up cartoon characters are great, but *test* the one you buy. They often stick and can be very frustrating.

Keeping It All Together

☐ Toy chests are attractive, but their heavy lids are dangerous. Smaller, open boxes or plastic wastebaskets or wicker baskets are better, and they're easy to cart around from room to room.

☐ Brightly painted wooden soda crates hung on a wall make attractive cubbies for holding small toys.

☐ Shoe bags made of transparent plastic are great for holding toys; everything is always visible. Hang one on the outside of a playpen to keep all those small toys organized.

☐ You can never have too many shelves in a child's room, but be sure they're hung securely. Do not hang them over baby's crib.

☐ A clothing closet is hardly necessary for an infant's room, since baby's clothes, even when hung up, take up so little room. Add shelves to clothing closets and store toys, clothing, diapers, and shoes there. The shelves can always be removed later on.

☐ Fix or discard broken toys as soon as they break or you'll never be able to keep up with the accumulated mess.

☐ Keep a lost and found box (a shoebox will do) in baby's room. When a small part of a larger toy becomes detached and you don't feel like searching for the missing part, just drop the toy into the box. You can make the repair when the rest of the toy turns up.

☐ Use a rake every night to get all of baby's toys into a corner. It's marvelous for a quick cleanup.

☐ Designate one kitchen or desk drawer as baby's drawer and fill it with her toys or with household objects that will amuse her, such as empty plastic bottles, key rings, old decks of cards, etc.

The Automatic Swing

Many parents consider the automatic swing a lifesaver. A few babies don't like it—mine didn't—but the majority do.

☐ Here's the easy way to put baby in the swing: With his back to you, hold him by the thighs and press his arms to his side with your arms so he won't grab the side bars. Then get *behind* the swing and slip him in from the back.

☐ For a very young baby who doesn't sit up yet, get the kind of swing with a reclining seat or cradle.

☐ Put baby in the swing right from the start. *"I put my first in it at four weeks, but I waited too long with my second and he never liked it,"* said one mother we interviewed.

☐ When introducing your baby to a swing, try putting him in only when he's in a cheerful mood. If he gets put in when he's fussy or crying, he may learn to hate the swing. Later on, when you know he enjoys swinging, it can be used to pacify him.

☐ Be careful. Baby swings can be tipped over, especially by large dogs or by very active older children.

Sibling Play

☐ Use the playpen and flexible corral for the *older* children. They can play with their toys inside and baby can't bother them.

☐ Put the infant seat in the shallow kiddie pool so that both baby and your children can enjoy the pool. Just be sure that you stay there to watch the baby.

☐ Hook baby's jumper toy onto the swing set so baby can be with the big kids. Supervise, though.

Places to Visit

Excursions can be fun no matter how young your baby is. Even if the baby is too young to take it all in, the change of scenery will do you both good. Consider visiting the following places, and do invite other parents and kids along:

☐ A construction site

☐ The children's room at the library

☐ A nearby farm (ask the owners if they wouldn't mind giving you a tour of the barn)

☐ A playground, naturally, but try a new one for a change

☐ Someone's office

☐ A museum or nature center

☐ A zoo or your local pet store

☐ A toy store.

Baby's Library

The following books were recommended over and over again by parents. Remember that it is never too early to start reading to a child. Babies pick up words and react to familiar sounds very early. You'll find, too, that reading to your baby can become an important, intimate experience. It will help both of you wind down at the end of the day.

> *Goodnight Moon* by Margaret Wise Brown (New York: Harper & Row, 1947).
>
> *Pat the Bunny* by Dorothy Kunhardt (Racine, Wisconsin: Western Publishing, 1962).
>
> *I am A Bunny* by Ole Risom, illustrated by Richard Scarry. (Racine, Wisconsin: Western Publishing, 1963).
>
> *The Me Book* by John E. Johnson (New York: Random House, 1979).
>
> *Kittens Are Like That* by Jan Pfloog (New York: Random House, 1976).
>
> *500 Words to Grow On* by Harry McNaught (New York: Random House, 1973).

For More Ideas

The following books are full of ideas and guidelines on amusing babies. Check your library for others.

> *What to Do When There's Nothing to Do* by members of the staff of the Boston Children's Medical Center and Elizabeth M. Gregg (New York: Dell, 1970).
>
> *How to Play with Your Children (and When Not To)* by Brian Sutton-Smith (New York: Hawthorn/Dutton, 1974).
>
> *Learningames for the First Three Years* by Joseph Sparling and Isabelle Lewis (New York: Walker and Co., 1978).
>
> *Games Babies Play* by Julie Hagstrom and Joan Morrill (New York: A & W Publishers, Inc., 1979).

11

Travel

General Observations

☐ Don't lug a lot of equipment along with you when you travel. Many towns have rental services from which you can get cribs, high chairs, strollers, etc.

☐ If you're visiting relatives or friends, ask them to find out beforehand what you can get there to make your stay more comfortable. They can look in the Yellow Pages under "Rentals."

☐ Ask the people you're visiting if they can borrow toys from neighbors. It helps a lot.

☐ If you're renting a cottage for your vacation, ask your landlord to help with whatever you need. One mother told us that such a request turned up a playpen and two reliable baby-sitters.

☐ If you have to improvise a bed for baby, use a blanket-lined dresser drawer. If she's too big for this, the floor is the safest place for baby.

☐ Use a backpack to carry all your traveling essentials: diapers, bottles, food, even your purse. If baby is small enough, carry him in a front pack so your hands are free.

☐ A harness and leash are much handier than a stroller when you're traveling. Not only are they easier for you to carry, but your child can get some exercise as you're changing planes, for example.

☐ If your baby is sitting well *and* if you're used to it, carrying a child on your back is great for traveling. Babies are almost always happy in the back carrier, and if you've got the kind that stands by itself, you can feed him in it, too. But *don't* make the mistake of buying a carrier and leaving the next day. You do have to build up your strength so that carrying it is easy.

☐ Don't put baby in a backpack until he's about five months old, when his neck will be strong enough to withstand all the bumping around. His neck might be injured if he's put in earlier.

☐ An umbrella used as a sun shield is very handy in hot tropical weather.

☐ If you are going to a sunny spot for your vacation, be sure to take a hat for baby and ask your doctor to recommend a good sunscreening lotion. Babies burn easily.

☐ For a day at the beach, bring an upright shopping cart and dump everything in it: umbrella, change of clothing, blankets, towels, food.

☐ Don't forget to take your first aid kit on vacation (see pp. 183–184).

☐ Take baby's night-light on vacation.

☐ From one mother: *"Since we did a lot of traveling, I encouraged both my children to become attached to blankets. That way, they'd always have something comforting in bed in a strange place. But blankets can be a nuisance during the day, so I decided to train my second child to feel secure with a little stuffed dog, too. It was easier to carry it around planes and airports."*

☐ If you usually leave your baby with one set of friends or relatives while you're away, leave a set of toys and other necessities with them permanently. These might include everything from bottles and diapers to an infant seat and playpen that can double as a bed.

☐ If you're taking baby's quilt along, make it double as a changing pad at airports, in taxis, etc. Cover it with an old pillow case, pin a long ribbon to it, roll it up, and tie as shown in the illustration at right, so you can carry it on your shoulder.

☐ Anticipate any time changes and begin to alter feeding and sleeping schedules a few days before the trip begins.

☐ A getaway weekend with a newborn is a great chance for new parents to get some exercise, rest, and good food. Try an inn or a ski lodge. Phone ahead to arrange the crib assembly *before* your arrival, and ask for strategic room placement away from other guest rooms. *But* don't expect a vacation with a baby to be a real vacation. It may be nice, but it won't really be all that restful unless you bring along a full-time sitter! Do remember that many hotels offer sitter services or will make arrangements with local sitters for you.

☐ Bring inflatable toys. They're light and take up practically

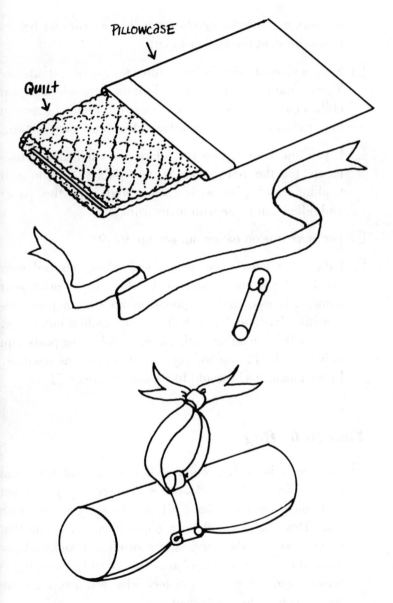

The Travel Quilt

no room at all. Inflatable beach balls are easier for babies to handle than the rubber kind.

☐ Keep a separate bag for necessities for use in restaurants. These would include a bottle; bib; moist towelettes; your child's eating utensils, if he uses any; a belt, in case you have to improvise your own high chair; and a toy or two.

☐ If you find youself in a restaurant and can't find amusements for the baby, look again. Babies love to tear napkins, and play with spoons and with the paper umbrellas that come with many drinks.

☐ For more tips on eating out see pp. 92–93

☐ Label your baby! You never know when you and your child will become separated. On long trips, print your name, address, and telephone number on a pressure-sensitive label and attach it to your child's outerwear. (One mother we talked with added the following postscript to her label: "Please find my parents as soon as possible. In the meantime, I would like some ice cream.")

Your Baby Bag

☐ Prepare a baby bag and you'll save lots of time and energy. Keep it by the door to grab every time you go out and you'll know you have all of baby's necessities with you. This "bag" could be a picnic hamper, a bag that hangs easily on the handles of a stroller, a backpack, or whatever fits your need. Change the contents according to season, and remember to restock what you use. Here are some suggestions for its contents:

- Diapers
- Diaper pins
- Plastic pants
- Disposable wet wipes, individually wrapped
- Plastic bags and ties for dirty diaper and wiper disposal
- Ointment for rash
- A few paper towels
- Purse-size tissue pack
- Two or more playthings—toys, small rattles books, etc. Change occasionally.
- Pacifier
- Change of clothes
- Sweater
- Pad to change baby on
- Damp washcloth with baking soda in a plastic bag. This will have to be changed frequently, but is wonderful for smelly spit-up on baby's clothes. Just sponge clothes with baking soda and the odor disappears.
- Bottles and nipples
- Food (See FOOD AND DRINK, pp. 149–150)
- Plastic or leather belt. If you eat out and the strap on the high chair is broken, or if your baby hops out of shopping carts, this will keep her secure. You could also buy a harness made for this purpose.
- Adhesive bandages
- Baby's security blanket (a duplicate)
- Masking tape. If the tabs on disposable diapers get wet and won't stick, use masking tape instead. Also, short pieces of masking tape will amuse baby during a traffic jam.

☐ In addition to having the above items on hand, you'll want to keep the following items in the car permanently (if you drive):
  - First aid kit (see pp. 183–184)
  - Blanket (for spur-of-the-moment picnics or for extra warmth)
  - Umbrella.

☐ Whether you're traveling by car, plane, boat, or train, you'll never regret taking a few minutes to plan and pack some surprises and distractions. Obviously, you'll be bringing more of these *new* things for longer trips. And they don't all have to be toys; household items work just as well. Here are some specific suggestions:
  - A purse you've stocked with keys, playing cards, a mirror, etc
  - A pad of paper and crayons
  - Pressure-sensitive dots for sticking on everything in sight
  - A book of cutouts—like glasses a child can put on—is very handy for amusement. Bring scissors, too. Or buy the punch-out type; scissors aren't needed.
  - Books about planes, buses, trains, boats—whatever you're on
  - Wind-up toys that make sounds or music boxes Avoid the ones that move about; there won't be too many surfaces on which to use them
  - A magazine to rip.

☐ Wrap whatever surprises you bring along. The excitement and suspense of unwrapping will get you through a good portion of the trip.

☐ Borrow what you can. *"My friends loaned me the toys I took. They were new to my daughter, and they worked fine,"* said one mother.

Food and Drink

Giving a baby something to eat or drink will often solve fussiness problems when you're out, so always have something on hand.

☐ See pp. 88–89 for a list of finger food that works well on trips.

☐ For long trips, freeze water and juice in plastic bottles. They'll be defrosted by the time you're ready to use them.

☐ Prepared and sealed formula bottles are much easier to take along, and there's no risk of spoilage due to lack of refrigeration. Be sure to check the expiration date, though.

☐ For babies drinking milk, just carry packets of powdered milk with you when traveling. You can mix it up fresh whenever baby wants it. Take your own water if you want to.

☐ Food that won't spoil—like crackers or rice cakes—is almost essential to stock in your baby bag when your baby is eating solids.

☐ A box of raisins will keep baby busy for a long time.

☐ If an older baby (over eighteen months) must have something to drink in the car and she won't take a bottle, use a special thermos bottle with an opening for a straw, or stick a straw into a narrow-necked plastic bottle—and hope. You might consider giving only water in the car. If it spills, at least it doesn't make a sticky mess.

Shopping with Baby

☐ Most infant seats and the General Motors infant car seat will fit into the shopping-cart seat area.

☐ When baby's really tiny, just pad the supermarket cart seat with blankets.

☐ If baby is just learning to sit, prop her up with two rolls of paper towels or toilet paper.

☐ A baby harness or plastic belt from a high chair or an old leather belt can be used as a safety belt in a supermarket cart if your child has a tendency to stand up in the cart.

In the Car

☐ Tie toys and bottles to the car seat with fairly short pieces of string. If they drop from baby's hands (and they will), they can easily be retrieved.

☐ Soft toys are best for the car. Sudden stops could dig sharp edges into baby's eyes or skin.

☐ Strap on the chest carrier *before* you get in the car (without baby in it, of course). When you get where you are going, you can pop baby in quickly.

☐ Tape a colorful picture where baby can see it. Change the picture frequently. It will give you lots to talk about with baby before he is old enough to look out of the windows.

☐ In the winter, loosen and/or remove some of baby's outer clothing after you put her in the car seat so she won't get too hot.

☐ The car radio is a wonderful distraction. Use it.

CAR SEATS

The best advice of all is: *Always put baby in a car seat*. No exceptions! And *always use your own seat belt*. (What would your baby do without *you?*) Here are some other tips:

☐ Get your infant car seat early, so you'll have something safe to put baby into when you come home from the hospital. Also, figure out beforehand how the thing works. You don't want to be standing outside the hospital door struggling with it with a newborn in your arms.

☐ Check to see if the car seat you're buying has undergone "dynamic testing," which means it has been tested under crash conditions. Federal safety standards have been inadequate when it comes to car seats. However, car seats manufactured after January 1, 1981, must meet federal standards, which require dynamic testing.

☐ Be sure your seat belts are compatible with the car seat your buying. Many seat belts in the backseat (especially in foreign cars) are too short to go around some car seats.

☐ If your car seat has an anchor or tether strap, you must attach it to the car. Otherwise it could harm your child in an accident. If it will be necessary for you to move the car seat often, buy one that does not require a tether.

☐ Be suspicious of car seats that are supposed to be okay for infants *and* toddlers. Chances are the needs of one are being met at the expense of the needs of the other.

☐ If your infant's head rolls around too much in the car seat, prop it up on either side with rolled-up cloth diapers.

☐ In summer, the metal parts on car seats can get hot enough to burn a child. To prevent this, cover the whole car seat with a large towel (or anything that covers it) every time you leave the car. It's not a bad idea to cover your own seat, too.

☐ In summer, put a cotton towel over the plastic seat to keep it cool and to absorb the baby's perspiration. Just cut holes in it for the straps to go through. Or buy a fitted cloth infant seat cover. These are sold in many stores that sell the seats.

☐ In winter, if baby cries and fusses in the car seat, try covering it with lamb's wool or some other soft, warm covering. The lamb's wool makes a big difference to some children.

☐ Car beds are not substitutes for car seats; they are not safe, as tests have shown. But they're very handy for motels, hotels, and friends' and relatives' houses, where there may not be adequate sleeping arrangements for babies.

☐ Beware of front-located, easy-to-undo clasps. You'd be surprised how quickly baby catches on.

☐ Keep the carton that the car seat comes in. Cut out a few windows and you'll have a little house your baby will love.

☐ If you have any questions about car seats and related gear, send them (along with a stamped, self-addressed long white envelope) to:

Physicians for Automotive Safety
50 Union Avenue
Irvington, New Jersey 17111.
For an additional 35 cents they will send you an informative booklet entitled, "Don't Risk Your Child's Life!"

☐ Send away for the free pamphlet entitled "Child Restraint Systems for Your Automobile" from:
Department of Transportation
National Highway Traffic Safety Administration
400 Seventh Street SW
Washington, D.C. 20590

☐ For a free copy of "Fact Sheet on Infant and Child Restraints," write to:
Governor's Traffic Safety Committee
Empire State Plaza
Albany, New York 12228

ON LONG CAR TRIPS

☐ Prepare baby's travel bag (see pp. 146–147).

☐ If you drive at night or start very early in the morning, baby will be asleep most of the time. (Note: This applies to infants in rear-facing, reclining car seats. It would not be advisable to make a child sleep sitting up all night in a car seat.)

☐ Help a toddler fill his own little lunch box and there should be no complaints about forgotten food.

☐ Frequent stops are very important. Infants up to six months need a chance to be hugged and physically played with, so don't just stick them in a high chair during rest stops. Older children need activity and a chance to stretch their muscles.

☐ It's ideal if someone can be in the back seat with the child to play with him. Finger games and songs amuse even very young children.

Airplane Travel

WHEN MAKING YOUR RESERVATION

☐ Tell them you're traveling with a baby, and take advantage of special services that may be offered (early boarding, bassinets, food and bottle warming, special children's menus, etc.).

☐ Ask if you can reserve the bulkhead seat (it's roomier). If you can't reserve one in advance, try to get to the airport early and see if you can make arrangements then.

☐ Find out the best times to fly—that is, the least busy times. You'll be most likely to get an empty seat for baby.

☐ In most cases, children under two fly for free but must share your seat. If there are empty seats on the flight, however, children are allowed to use them. You can reserve a seat for a child under two. You will be charged the Standard Child's rate; it generally costs two-thirds to three-quarters of the adult fare.

☐ If you plan to reserve a seat for your baby, find out whether your infant seat or car seat will be allowed on the plane. Also, since plane seat dimensions vary, check whether the seat you plan to bring will fit.

☐ If you are planning to take a stroller to use at stopovers, find out if you'll have to check these items with your luggage. Many airlines will not let you bring a stroller on the plane. You might consider a chest or backpack-type baby carrier or a harness instead.

☐ Find out ahead of time whether the airports you're flying to and from have special "nurseries" where you can change, nurse, and relax with your baby. Most large airports have them.

AT THE AIRPORT

☐ Find a window with a good view of the planes and trucks. There is a *lot* of activity at an airport that will amuse a child.

☐ Locate the nursery. Change, feed, and relax with the baby.

☐ Make sure the airline attendant at the gate knows you're with a baby. The airline will probably want you to board first and get settled.

ON THE PLANE

☐ Always nurse, bottle feed, or give a pacifier to your baby when your plane is taking off or landing. The sucking and swallowing relieves the pressure on baby's ears and makes him much more comfortable. If baby no longer takes a bottle, give snacks or liquid with a straw.

☐ Bring out the traveling baby bag when other distractions won't work (see pp. 146–147).

☐ For a very long plane ride, your doctor may recommend

some kind of medication for nausea, like Dramamine. Check this with the doctor.

☐ The best distraction on a plane for children about eighteen months or older is other children. Trade seats with other passengers or walk up and down the aisles to find some.

☐ Help yourself to the air sickness bag supplied on the plane. These are good to have back home in the baby's room. Keep them handy at all times. If you're fast enough, you'll save yourself a lot of trouble!

12

Baby-sitters

Finding Baby-sitters

☐ Always try to get sitters with references, preferably through families you know.

☐ If you respond to sitters' ads in the newspapers or on local bulletin boards, check references thoroughly. Be suspicious if you are asked to call them at specific times.

☐ Boys make fine baby-sitters, too. Check references and use your judgment as you would with anyone else.

☐ The following may serve as sources for baby-sitters:

- Local bulletin boards
- High school and college placement offices
- The local senior citizen's organizations
- Church groups
- 4-H Club leaders.
- The local hospital (for volunteers and retired nurses).

☐ Try to locate a baby-sitting pool or co-op. Generally, this is how they work: Member parents commit to a specified

number of hours during which they sit for other people's children. They are paid in coupons that are redeemable for the baby-sitting services of other member parents. The advantages of a co-op are that it's cheap—free, actually—and that you'll be getting mature sitters each time. The disadvantages are that you will have to baby-sit for other children and that you will probably always get a different sitter when you need one. (If you can't locate such a co-op in your area, consider starting one, even if it's on a limited scale. It's a great way to meet other parents!)

Leaving Baby for the First Time

It will probably be harder on you than on the baby when you leave for the first time. Here are some suggestions that may make it easier:

- [ ] Use relatives or close friends whom baby is familiar with.

- [ ] Let baby play with the sitter once or twice while you're there before leaving them alone.

- [ ] Have the baby-sitter come early so that you can show her around and get the baby used to her in your presence before you go.

- [ ] Go someplace nearby and don't stay long. This will make you feel better—the baby probably won't care.

- [ ] Call as often as you like to check on how things are going. Again, this is for *your* benefit.

When the Sitter Arrives

☐ You might want to state the following rules:

- No smoking
- No alcoholic beverages
- No visitors
- No tying up the phone.

☐ Use the following checklist of general information that you'll want the sitter to have. (Basic emergency information should be left *in writing* in the form of a copy of p. 162.) Write down as much of the following information as is appropriate. Keep copies for future use.

- Any special health problems the baby might have
- Baby's schedule (feeding, sleeping, etc.)
- Baby's special fears
- Baby's current mischief (such as "eats lint") and development ("stands up but can't sit down")
- Baby's special routine ("leave night light on," "wind up musical mobile before bedtime," etc.)
- Layout of the house
- Location of all baby supplies
- Stove operation, if necessary
- Operation of TV, stereo, etc.
- Whereabouts and habits of pets
- How door locks work and location of extra keys (in case a bathroom door gets locked, for instance)
- Expected deliveries or visitors
- How to handle phone calls (A sitter should never give out your whereabouts or tell when exactly you are expected home.).

☐ Your baby-sitter should also be given the following emergency-related information:

- Location of fuse box or circuit breaker and how it works
- Location of flashlights
- Location and operation of fire extinguisher
- Operation of fire/smoke and burglar alarm
- Fire escape routes
- Instructions for common childhood emergencies (see pp. 185–194) or a copy of *Standard First Aid and Personal Safety* by the American National Red Cross (Garden City, N.Y.: Doubleday, 1975).

☐ Have the baby-sitter spend some time with the baby before you leave so that you can observe him or her diapering the baby, playing with her, etc.

General Observations

☐ Get your child used to baby-sitters from the beginning; you'll have trouble introducing them later on if you don't.

☐ Although your baby may scream as you leave, rest assured that he will probably stop shortly after you leave. If you're really worried, you can remain *out of sight* until the crying stops. Or, better yet, call later to see how things are going. The trick is to *act with confidence!*

☐ Whenever possible, use the same sitter. The fewer faces your baby has to get accustomed to, the easier it will be.

☐ For a little extra money, you may be able to get an ambitious sitter to do some chores, such as folding laundry, washing dishes, dusting, etc.

Baby-sitter's Information Sheet

Make copies of this page and keep them by your phone. Before you make copies, however, fill in everything except the information about where you'll be, which you will fill in each time you leave.

I am at_____
        (name)

_____
        (address)

_____
        (phone)

I will be back at_____

You are at
this address_____

sitting for_____

Doctor_____

_____
        (phone)

Backup
Doctor_____

_____
        (phone)

Hospital_____

_____
        (phone)

Neighbor_____

_____
        (phone)

Phone Call
Messages:_____

_____

_____

Police_____

Fire_____

Ambulance_____

Poison Control Center_____

All-Night Drug Store_____

Taxi_____

Special Instructions:

_____

_____

_____

_____

Your Baby-sitter List

Have the names of your baby-sitters all in one place. If one is
not available, just call the next on your list. It's also helpful
to put down what times they are free, like "only on Friday
nights" or "weekday afternoons." It will save you some
calling time.

Name   *Phone Number*   *When Available*

_____

_____

_____

_____

_____

_____

_____

_____

_____

_____

_____

_____

_____

_____

☐ Have the sitter introduce a new toy that you've stashed just for this occasion. Or if a special treat—such as a favorite dessert—is on the agenda, have the baby-sitter offer it.

☐ If the sitter isn't coming until after the baby has gone to sleep, make sure that the baby is at least familiar with the sitter. Your baby may get frightened if she wakes up and finds a stranger there.

☐ Don't confine sitter services to evenings when you are out. Consider using them for a few hours each week just so you can spend some time alone pampering yourself. You might want to hire someone to take the baby out while you stay home.

☐ Here's a great gift that will benefit both you and the sitter: A copy of *The Complete Babysitter's Handbook*, by Carol Barkin and Elizabeth James (New York: Simon and Schuster, 1980).

☐ Write or call the U.S. Consumer Product Safety Commission (see p. 65) for a free copy of an informative booklet entitled, "The Super Sitter."

13

Working Mothers

All mothers work, of course, but this chapter will deal with mothers who work at something besides motherhood and must find ways to care for their children while they work.

Going Back to Work

☐ The question of when to return to work must be the most often-asked question among new mothers who wish to continue working. And the most common answer is a frustrating one: It's up to you. Some women reported that they couldn't wait to return to work and went back as early as one month after the birth. Others said that they enjoyed the opportunity to take a year off and see "how the other half lives." Here are some questions that may help you make the decision:
- Can you arrange for suitable child care?
- Do you physically and mentally feel up to returning to work?
- Will your career suffer if you don't return immediately?

- How will your household fare financially?
- Does your baby have any problems that require special care? If so, can these needs be met by any other care giver?
- What do you really *want* to do?

☐ You're likely to feel like an outsider on your first days back at work. Try to get involved in what others have been doing in your absence instead of inundating them with baby pictures and stories of the birth.

☐ Don't crowd your desk with baby pictures—no matter how cute your baby is. You don't want to be thought of as "Mommy" at work.

☐ Keep a special card in your Rolodex or in your desk that contains all your child-care-related telephone numbers including backup care, so that if there's an emergency at home you can take care of it quickly.

☐ Make sure that whoever answers your phone is familiar with the name of your child's care giver, so that if there is a problem at home, the call will be put through to you immediately.

Nursing and Working

☐ Even when you've expressed twenty ounces of milk, it's wisest to leave some formula with the sitter as well, in case she runs out.

☐ Pump your breasts at work (even if you have to throw the milk away) to keep up the milk supply.

☐ Said one mother, *"Expressing milk at the office took too*

*much time and was too anxiety provoking. Somehow my
breasts adjusted to a week and weekend schedule."*

Full- or Part-Time Care Givers

☐ If you want to locate one, try:
- Advertising, not only in the local paper but by signs at supermarkets, community centers, etc.
- Agencies
- A senior citizen center
- Local colleges
- Churches and synagogues
- Telling *everyone* you know, and even people you don't know (like shopkeepers), that you're looking for someone. Good recommendations can come from unexpected sources.

☐ If you don't know what to offer as a salary, call an agency to find out its rates. Bear in mind that agencies charge more than anyone else.

☐ If you place an ad in the paper, you'll probably get a lot of calls and have to initially screen the candidates over the phone. If you want to find out more about them without commiting yourself, say "I'm seeing someone today I'll probably hire, but why don't you tell me about yourself, and if this person doesn't work out, I'll call you back for an interview."

☐ When you're interviewing someone to look after baby in your home, make sure you leave them alone together for a little while, while you get coffee or do something else. Observe whether your prospect attempts to play with the baby.

☐ Don't be afraid to trust your feelings about the people you're interviewing. Don't let your head by turned by a lot of recommendations and qualifications. If you're not instinctively comfortable with the person you hire, you're going to worry about your child.

☐ Look for someone who will play with and stimulate your baby. Don't settle for a custodian.

☐ If you have several possible choices, hire each for a trial day or two. Go in and out of the house that day. You'll learn a lot.

☐ Spend several days with the sitter and the baby before you go back to work. The sitter will not be a sudden stranger to your baby, and she will have learned about the baby and the baby's routine directly from you.

☐ If the baby-sitter you like is firm about schedules and you're not, don't worry too much. Babies seem to do exactly what the sitter wants and never what the mother wants.

☐ Be sure to give your baby's caretaker a notorized slip allowing her to care for your child in a medical emergency. Sample:

_____has my permission to authorize
any emergency medical treatment in my absence.

Doctor_____

Phone_____

Hospital_____

                    Signed_____

Day-Care Centers

☐ Observe as many of these as you can before you make your choice. Here are some things to look for:

- Will the people who take care of your baby be there most of the time, or will personnel constantly change?
- What are the qualifications of the staff?
- Do the care givers seem to genuinely love children?
- Are the attitudes of the care givers the same as yours in regard to interactive play, feeding on demand as opposed to a set schedule, nutrition, etc.?
- Will there be varied activities available to your child as she grows?
- What is the general atmosphere of the center? Is it homey and cheerful or large and institutional? Would *you* want to spend an entire day there?

☐ If your baby is going to be exposed to other children, he'll be exposed to lots of germs! You can expect your child to catch any and all bugs when he starts a day-care program—something he would go through eventually, anyway. The point is: Be sure to arrange for backup child care if your baby must stay home. And don't get discouraged—your baby *will*, eventually, build up a resistance to colds.

☐ You'll want to keep your child's belongings clearly marked so that you're not always having to replace them. Order a rubber stamp with your child's name so that you can make your own labels, using pressure-sensitive adhesive labels. Use these for labeling toys, bottles, food containers, and anything else you have to send along.

☐ When sending your child to a day-care center, you'll have to send along lots of changes of clothing. Make these the cheapest ones available—or, better yet, look for used clothing at garage sales. Often, these clothes will hardly get used before your baby graduates to the next size.

☐ Try to contact parents of children who attend the same day-care center. If problems come up, they will be more easily solved if they are shared. And you may be able to work out a co-op transportation plan.

☐ If you are suspicious or unhappy about any aspect of your child's treatment, don't be afraid to speak up.

☐ Stay in constant touch with day-care personnel to find out how your baby is doing, what she is eating, when she is sleeping, etc. It's so easy to fall into the habit of letting others take over completely.

☐ Check out the group child-care programs described in *The New Extended Family: Day Care That Works* by Ellen Galinsky and William H. Hooks (Boston: Houghton Mifflin, 1977).

☐ Get a copy of a booklet entitled, "A Parent's Guide to Day Care," published in 1980 by the U.S. Department of Health and Human Services, Administration for Children, Youth and Families, Day Care Division. It is available from:

> Superintendent of Documents
> U.S. Government Printing Office
> Washington, D.C. 20402

Working at Home

☐ It's hard to work at home and have a sitter and baby there, too. You're bound to bump into each other, and when baby sees you, she'll want you.

☐ Allow your child to be a part of your work. Even tiny ones can go with you to mail envelopes. Toddlers can stick on stamps, take copies from a copying machine, gather loose paper clips, etc.

☐ For days when there's no sitter and you have to work:

- Provide the child with the tools of your trade (toy typewriter, telephone, erasers, etc.) so he can imitate Mommy, and more importantly, so that he won't demand *your* things.
- Have special toys in your office that she plays with only there.
- Keep a TV in your office and share special shows like *Sesame Street* or *Mister Rogers' Neighborhood*. You don't have to pay full attention, but you can react occasionally or answer questions.
- Keep a purse filled with safe things to discover (or any other super distraction) for those times when you get an important phone call.

General Observations

☐ Count on a lot of hysterical acting-out once you get home after work. It's been saved up all day with the sitter. Testing, anger, and other guilt-inducing behavior is developmentally normal and occurs with all children—not only those of working mothers.

☐ If you have to drive a long way to work, consider leaving baby with a sitter near your job rather than near your home. You get more time with the baby this way during the rides to and from work.

☐ Try to keep your weekends as free as possible. You'll need the time to catch up on family needs, chores, and just plain relaxing. Be firm when explaining this to friends and relatives.

☐ When your child gets older, bring him to work with you on occasion so that he can see exactly what goes on.

☐ Try to contact other working mothers in your business or industry to find out what problems they share and which solutions work best.

14

Your Child's Safety

Around the House in General

☐ Before baby starts crawling, get down on the floor and get a baby's-eye view of your house. It's a revelation—you'll see all sorts of hazardous stuff that you wouldn't have noticed before.

☐ As soon as babies can move about, they can get into things you would not believe. Therefore, do not let them out of your sight! *Especially* in those first heady months of independent movement.

☐ All empty electrical outlets in walls should be filled with blank plastic plugs.

☐ Tack down or tape all loose wires and cords.

☐ Sharp corners of tables can be covered with special plastic safety devices available in hardware stores.

☐ Keep babies away from matches, lighters, and cigarettes.

☐ Plastic bags can suffocate babies. Never allow them to be played with. Dispose of them out of baby's reach.

- [ ] Do not let your baby play near waste paper baskets or garbage pails.

- [ ] Put soft plastic covers over doorknobs so that your baby can't turn them.

- [ ] Forget safety locks, especially if you have other children around. *Someone* will forget to lock. Put dangerous and poisonous items out of reach, or lock them up in a special box.

- [ ] If the doors in your house or apartment have locks, remove them. If you must have locks on any doors, make sure you have spare keys that can be used to unlock them from the outside.

- [ ] Put valuable objects on high shelves to prevent breakage.

- [ ] Put colored decals on glass doors at your child's eye level so she'll notice the glass.

- [ ] Don't keep anything in front of a window that a child can use to climb out the window.

- [ ] Windows should have screens, gates, or window guards.

- [ ] If they do not, open from the top only.

- [ ] Put "tot-finder" decals on baby's window facing outside. These let firemen know instantly which rooms might contain helpless children. You can usually get them free from your local fire department.

- [ ] Never leave a carriage near a stairway, driveway, or ramp. Use the brake when you're not moving the carriage.

- [ ] If you use a wooden folding gate (the kind with diamond-shaped openings) in front of a doorway, remember that children may easily learn to climb them.

☐ Turn the water temperature down in your home so baby won't accidentally be scalded. 130°F or 55°C is safe.

☐ Keep a list of emergency telephone numbers (see the form on p. 216) at *each* telephone extension in your home.

☐ Don't wax your floors.

☐ Never leave animals and babies alone together.

☐ Pick up the magazines your child loves to scatter all over the floor. They're easy for toddlers to slip on.

☐ If you answer the door or the phone, take baby with you. In the time it takes to go to the door, babies can swallow poison or climb a bookcase and fall off.

☐ Teach your baby to open her mouth when you ask. Make it a game. That way, if you ever have to retrieve a small object from his mouth, he'll be able to cooperate. (Your pediatrician will be grateful, too!)

☐ Never leave a baby alone in a bathroom or kitchen.

☐ Never give food to a child if you will not be present to watch him eat it. Children can choke too easily.

☐ Use dimmer switches in baby's room and in hallways so that you'll always have "instant night lights" if you need them.

☐ If you know of a product intended for use by children that seems unsafe to you, write to the U.S. Consumer Product Safety Commission, Washington, D.C. 20207.

☐ See pp. 150–153 for tips on auto safety.

In the Kitchen

☐ If you use safety locks in the kitchen for your drawers leave one baby-level drawer open so your child won't be entirely frustrated. Fill it with safe kitchen items—plastic margarine tubs, wooden spoons—and change regularly so there are new surprises to find.

☐ Use plastic cups and dishes (or even paper plates, if you don't mind the expense) rather than breakable ones for babies.

☐ Teach babies early to stay away from the stove—whether it's on or not.

☐ Avoid tableclothes. Babies love to grab.

☐ Get into the habit of reading directions on all containers. This applies to household cleaning products as well as food. "Refrigerate after opening" means just that.

☐ Unused refrigerators and freezers should be stored with doors removed.

☐ Turn all pot and pan handles toward the back of the stove so that a baby can't grab them. Use the back burners as much as possible.

☐ If control knobs on the stove can be reached by your child, remove them when you're not using them.

In the Bathroom

☐ Don't leave bath mats on the floor in front of the tub. Toddlers can trip or skid on them and hit their heads on the tub. Even the rubber-backed mats are unsafe.

☐ Be sure the rubber mat in the bathtub covers the whole bottom.

☐ Throw a towel over the bathroom door to keep babies from slamming it shut and possibly getting locked in.

In the Nursery

☐ Do not allow food in baby's crib or playpen. Crumbs will attract bugs.

☐ After you've pulled the side of the crib up, always give it a hard push down to make sure it's secure.

☐ If you put a trapeze-type exerciser in the crib, make sure that the mattress is low enough that if the baby crawls under it, he won't get his neck caught.

☐ Place baby's crib away from windows, lamps, and other electrical appliances.

☐ Do not use a crib that doesn't meet the Consumer Product Safety Commission's standards (see pp. 56–57).

☐ Babies don't need pillows for sleeping. If you keep stuffed animals in the crib, keep them small and light.

At Staircases

☐ Light stairs well and keep them free of toys and clutter.

☐ Use gates at top *and bottom* of stairs.

☐ Tie a rope under the banister so kids will have something to hold on to when they're learning to walk up and down.

☐ Put your bottom stair gate three stairs up and let baby practice going up and down those three stairs.

☐ You can have gates made to match your wrought-iron railing. (Check the Yellow Pages under "Foundries" or "Iron Works.") Just be sure the bars are close enough together so baby's head or body can't get stuck. (Bars should be no more than 2⅜ inches apart.)

☐ As early as possible, teach baby to go up and down stairs safely.

☐ It's a good idea to have carpeting on your stairs.

Poisons

☐ Keep all dangerous substances in their original containers.

☐ Always return poisonous products to their appropriate places *immediately* after use.

☐ More and more manufacturers are making poisonous products available in child-resistant packages. Buy these whenever possible.

☐ Products that are intended for the same purpose (such as dishwashing detergents) often vary in their degree of poison content. When you have a choice, buy the safest, mildest product.

☐ Children usually have good associations with pleasantly scented products and will be more prone to eat and/or drink them. When you can, buy poisonous products that are not scented.

☐ Avoid products that come in aerosol cans.

☐ Explain to children as early as possible, and in whatever manner is necessary, that poisons are harmful and that children should stay away from them.

☐ Here are some items that are commonly found in most homes and should be kept out of children's reach:

Acids	Kerosene
Aerosols	Mace (chemical)
Ammonia	Model cement
Antiseptics	Mouthwash
Aspirin	Nail polish
Bathroom bowl cleaner	Nail polish remover
Benzene	Narcotics
Bleach	Oven cleaner
Bubble bath	Paint
Cigarettes	Paint thinner
Cleaning fluids	Permanent wave solution
Cologne	Pesticides
Copper and brass cleaners	Petroleum distillates
Corn and wart removers	Pine oil
Dishwasher detergents	Plants
Drain cleaners	Rodenticides
Drugs	Shampoo
Eye makeup	Shaving lotion
Fertilizers	Silver polish
Furniture polish	Strychnine
Garden chemicals	Turpentine
Glue	Typewriter cleaner fluid
Hair dyes	Vitamins
Insecticides	Window wash solvent
Iodine	

☐ Send away for the free pamplet "Preventing Childhood Poisonings" from:

> Food and Drug Administration
> Office of Consumer Affairs
> Consumer Communications Staff
> 5600 Fishers Lane
> Rockville, Maryland 20857

POISONOUS PLANTS

☐ The following plants are poisonous, either in terms of minor irritations or in terms of poisoning of the system. Avoid them, no matter how pretty they look in your home or garden. If your baby swallows *any* part of *any* plant, call the Poison Control Center immediately.

Angel's trumpet
Apple tree
Autumn crocus
Baneberry
Belladonna lilly
Black locust
Bleeding heart
Bloodroot
Buttercup
Caladium
Castor bean
Cherry tree
Chinaberry tree
Christmas rose
Cowslip
Daffodil
Daphne
Deadly amanita

Death camas
Dieffenbachia
Elderberry
Elephant's ear
English holly
English ivy
False hellebore
Fig tree
Fly agaric mushroom
Four o'clock
Foxglove
Golden chain
Horse chestnut tree
Hyacinth
Hydrangea
Inkberry
Iris
Jack-in-the-pulpit

Lady's slipper
Lantana
Larkspur
Lily of the valley
Lupine
Mayapple
Milkweed
Mistletoe
Monkshood
Moonseed
Morning glory
Mountain laurel
Narcissus
Nettle
Nightshade
Oleander
Peach tree
Philodendron

Poinsettia
Poison hemlock
Poison ivy
Poison oak
Pokeweed
Potato (eyes, stems,
    spoiled parts)
Privet
Rhododendron
Rhubarb
Rosary pea
Skunk cabbage

Snakeroot
Sneezeweed
Snow-on-the-mountain
Snowdrop
Sour dock
Sweet pea
Tobacco
Tomato (leaves)
Water hemlock
Wisteria
Yellow jasmine
Yew

First Aid Supplies for Babies

Check your supplies periodically and restock when necessary:

- Assorted sizes of adhesive bandages
- 3″ sterile gauze squares (for larger cuts and scrapes)
- 1″ and 2″ rolls of sterile gauze bandages (for holding gauze dressings in place)
- 1″ adhesive tape (for holding dressings or bandages in place)
- Roll of sterile absorbent cotton or sterile cotton balls
- Baby scissors (for cutting baby's fingernails and toenails)
- Scissors (for cutting bandages and dressings to size)
- Cotton-tipped swabs (for applying ointments—*never* use in ears or nose)
- Rectal thermometer
- Tweezers (for removing splinters)

- Syrup of ipecac (to induce vomiting)
- Activated charcoal (to absorb poison)
- Epsom salts (strong laxative)
- Rubbing alcohol

} FOR USE IN CASE OF POISONING. USE ONLY AS DIRECTED BY PHYSICIAN OR POISON CONTROL CENTER.

- Hydrogen peroxide (3 percent solution—for cleaning wounds and soaking bandages off)
- Antibiotic ointment (bacitracin or Neosporin—to prevent infections in cuts)
- Petroleum jelly (to help prevent diaper rash)
- Diaper rash ointment or powder (such as Desitin, A and D Ointment, Caldesene)
- Baby aspirin or Tylenol or liquid acetaminophen (to use as directed for fever, pain—easy to give to infants in liquid form)
- Bicarbonate of soda (Baking soda—to use for heat rash, to relieve itching)
- Calomine lotion (to relieve itching)
- Nasal syringe (to extract mucus from baby's nose)
- Hot-water bottle (to relieve stomach ache, earache, etc.)
- Pedialyte (for use as directed by doctor for liquid replacement during diarrhea)
- Antiseptic (ask your doctor for recommendation)
- Ginger ale or cola drink (some doctors recommend for upset stomachs)
- Vaporizer or humidifier

KEEP ALL SUPPLIES OUT OF THE REACH OF CHILDREN!

First Aid for Emergencies and Minor Accidents

These first aid procedures are not intended as a substitute for a doctor's care, but they will help you cope with a crisis before you can reach a doctor or other medical assistance. Please read these instructions now and familiarize yourself with them.

Some especially important procedures have been marked this way: ■; they call for immediate action on your part. As a responsible parent, you should study what to do *now*, before an accident happens. You do not want to have to read about choking as your child is turning blue.

The best advice is: *Don't panic, stay calm*. This will not only help you cope quickly and sensibly, but also reassure and calm your child.

ABRASIONS

☐ First soak in warm, soapy water. Gently clean the scraped skin. Be sure to remove any loose particles of dirt.

☐ Apply hydrogen peroxide, then an antibiotic ointment or cream.

☐ Cover the scrape with a sterile dressing.

☐ If the dirt is too deep for you to remove painlessly, ask your doctor to do it using a local anesthetic.

BEE OR OTHER INSECT STINGS

■ If the child begins to have any difficulty breathing, she must have medical care immediately. Rush to the nearest doctor or hospital emergency room. Call the police and get them to drive you there if necessary. They may be able to administer some emergency measures as well. (Some children have an allergic reaction to stings that causes their throats to swell. They must be treated quickly before they suffocate.)

■ If any other allergic reactions appear (for example, hives or vomiting), call your doctor right away.

☐ Relieve the itch or sting with ice cubes, Calomine lotion, a paste of bicarbonate of soda (mix the powder with a few drops of water), or vinegar. If it's a bee sting, remove the stinger by scraping it out with a tweezer cleaned with alcohol or soap and water.

BITES

Animal

☐ Control bleeding if necessary. (See CUTS, pp. 190–191.)

☐ Wash thoroughly with soap and water and cover with sterile bandage.

☐ Call your pediatrician.

☐ The animal must be tested for rabies, so either keep track of it or call the police to help capture it.

Human

☐ Same treatment as for animal bites if the skin is broken. Don't forget to call the doctor.

BREATHING: ARTIFICIAL RESPIRATION

■ Get someone else to summon medical help. (Call the police, then your doctor.)

■ Proceed *only* if child is *not* breathing.

■ Clear the child's mouth of debris with your finger. Be careful not to push any possible obstruction into her throat.

■ With the child on his back, place your hand under his neck and gently tip his head back to open the air passage. Chin must be *up*.

■ With your ear to the child's mouth, listen for breathing to begin. If it does not:

■ Cover the child's mouth and nose with your mouth and puff *some* air into the child's mouth. His lungs are much smaller than yours, so use only a partial breath.

■ Put your ear to the child's mouth and listen for air coming out.

• *If air comes out:*

Continue gently breathing into his lungs at a rate of about one new breath every three to five seconds.

Take your mouth away between breaths to allow air to be expelled.

Keep this up until the child can breathe by himself.

• *If no air comes out:*

Try another breath. Watch the chest to see if it rises. If no air is getting into the lungs, there may be a throat obstruction.

Remove obstruction. See CHOKING, p. 189.

Return the child onto his back. Tilt his head again to point the chin up.

Begin artificial respiration again. (See column at left.)

BUMPS AND BRUISES

☐ Relieve the pain with an ice cube (wrapped in a cloth or a plastic bag) and a kiss.

BURNS

Serious burns (Third degree: resulting in white or charred skin or extensive second-degree burns.)

■ If clothes catch fire, roll the child in something to smother the flames (a coat, a blanket, a rug, a tablecloth).

■ Never let a child run with burning clothes.

■ Cover burned skin with a clean cloth or a sheet.

☐ Get medical help immediately. (Rush to the nearest physician or emergency room; call the police if you need transportation.)

☐ Treat for shock. See SHOCK, pp. 193–194.

Minor burns (First and second degree: resulting in red skin and/or blisters)

■ Run cold water over burned skin immediately (or apply wet cold compresses). Continue until pain subsides. And for anything but very minor burns, seek medical attention right away.

☐ Cover burned skin with a sterile bandage.

☐ Do not apply any ointment (first aid creams, sprays, butter, grease, etc.) to burns.

☐ Do not pop blisters.

CHOKING

■ Never interfere with a baby's own attempts to cough or clear her own throat. If she can breathe, observe her carefully, but leave her alone.

☐ If baby can breathe but cannot dispel the object he's swallowed, get medical help immediately.

☐ If you can see the object, pull it out. Be careful not to push it farther down the throat.

To remove obstruction if the child cannot breathe:

■ Place the child head down over your knees. Give three or four sharp blows between the shoulder blades with the heel of your hand.

■ If the obstruction is not ejected, get behind the child and wrap your arms around his middle. Make a fist with one hand and cover it with the other. Place your fist between the ribs and the navel and thrust upward sharply four times. Repeat procedure if necessary.

☐ Administer artificial respiration if necessary. (See BREATHING: ARTIFICIAL RESPIRATION, pp. 186–187.)

CROUP

Croup without fever

■ Take the child into the bathroom and run hot water in the shower to make steam. Or, if it's cool outside (50° or less), bundle baby up and take him outside. Both methods should stop spasms.

■ If breathing does *not* improve after a few minutes, call police for emergency aid or rush to the nearest emergency room.

☐ After regular breathing is restored, humidify air in baby's room with vaporizer or humidifier. Baby should breathe moist air for several nights after croup.

Croup with fever

■ Call pediatrician for instructions. See above methods for making breathing easier for the child. If you are not able to reach a doctor quickly and have a breathing emergency, call police or rush to the nearest emergency room.

CUTS

Wounds Bleeding Severely

■ Any large flow of blood must be stopped immediately.

■ Cover the wound with a sterile or clean cloth (or just your hand if nothing else is available) and press the wound with your hand to control bleeding.

■ Still pressing, raise the injured part of the body higher than the heart if possible.

■ When bleeding is under control, bandage the wound firmly.

☐ Seek medical care immediately.

Minor Cuts and Scratches

☐ Control bleeding. (See above instructions.)

☐ Wash carefully with hydrogen peroxide or soap and water to remove all dirt.

☐ Apply an antibiotic ointment and bandage cut to keep dirt out.

DROWNING

■ Have someone else get medical help immediately.

■ Drain water from the lungs by tilting body head down for about eight to ten seconds.

■ Administer artificial respiration. (See BREATHING: ARTIFICIAL RESPIRATION, FAINTING, pp. 186–187.)

FEBRILE CONVULSIONS (Convulsions caused by high fever)

■ Cool child off quickly. Douse under cold running water, clothes and all.

■ Stay with child. Have someone else call a doctor immediately; if this is not possible, wrap child in a wet towel and make the call yourself.

■ If convulsions continue after a minute or two, call police or rush to emergency room. Do not wait to hear from the doctor.

FEVER

☐ If fever is over 101°, call your doctor.

■ If you can't reach the doctor and the fever has reached 103° or more, it should be brought down. Use this method: Bathe the child in lukewarm water in a tub, or give a sponge bath, for twenty minutes or so. Do not let the child get chilled. Dry quickly and thoroughly. Take temperature again. In necessary, repeat bath routine. Try to reach the doctor again.

FALLS

See HEAD INJURIES, below.

FRACTURES

☐ Call your doctor immediately.

☐ Until receiving instructions, do not move the child if she is reasonably comfortable.

☐ If the child must be moved, use a splint to keep the inured limb from moving.

☐ Apply an ice pack to reduce swelling.

HEAD INJURIES

■ If a child is unconscious or bleeding, call your doctor immediately. Control bleeding, but do not move the child.

☐ If a child is conscious, a cold compress will reduce swelling and pain of bruises. Call your doctor for further instructions.

NOSEBLEED

☐ Keep the child quiet and still. He can sit or lie down, but make sure the blood drains out rather than down the throat by having him lean forward slightly or lie on his side.

☐ Put a key or coin or other cold object on the back of his neck.

POISON (SWALLOWED)

■ Call poison control center immediately and follow exact instructions. If you can't reach the center, call your doctor.

■ If you can't reach instant medical help on the phone, and the child is conscious, give one or two glasses of milk (or water) to dilute the poison. Rush to nearest hospital.

POISON OR CHEMICAL ON SKIN

■ Rinse with water immediately. Call your doctor.

PUNCTURE WOUNDS

☐ Control bleeding if necessary. (See CUTS, pp. 190–191).

☐ Clean well with soap and water. Bandage.

☐ Call the pediatrician. She or he may want to give a tetanus booster shot.

SHOCK

☐ Always treat a child for shock if an injury is serious.

■ Shock symptoms: The child may be weak, cold, pale, sweaty, breathing quickly but shallowly, or nauseous.

■ Treatment: Lay her down. Cover her lightly with a blanket. Keep her warm, but do not overheat. Put a pillow under her legs to raise them ten to twelve inches.

☐ Stay with the child and comfort her. Do not give her anything to eat or drink.

☐ Call your pediatrician.

SPLINTERS

☐ Soak the skin in soapy water.

☐ Use tweezers cleaned with alcohol to remove the splinter.

☐ Wash the opening.

☐ If the splinter is too large or deep for you to remove, see your doctor.

SPRAINS

☐ Keep child quiet and elevate for at least a half an hour to reduce swelling.

☐ Keep ice pack on sprain.

☐ Call your doctor. If there is pain and/or swelling, the injured limb should be examined by a doctor.

STINGS

☐ See BEE OR OTHER INSECT STINGS, pp. 185–186.

SWALLOWED SMALL OBJECTS

☐ See CHOKING, p. 189.

Free Things

Send away for the following free pamphlets on the subject of child safety:
"Child Safety"
Safety Now Company
P.O. Box 567, Department FS
Jenkintown, Pennsylvania 19046

☐ Safety information on toys and other baby products is availble from the U.S. Consumer Product Safety Commission, Washington, D.C. 20207.
Or call their toll-free hotline:
(800) 638-8326 (Continental U.S.)
(800) 492-8363 (Maryland residents only)
(800) 638-8333 (Alaska, Hawaii, Puerto Rico, Virgin Islands)

15

Health

General Observations

☐ Take the responsibility of keeping your *own* record of the shots and vaccines your baby receives. (See YOUR CHILD'S IMMUNIZATION CHART AND HEALTH RECORD, pp. 204–205.)

☐ When you move, ask your pediatrician to let you have your baby's records instead of mailing them in case you have an emergency before you've chosen a new pediatrician.

☐ If your baby has been treated by a doctor other than your own in an emergency, be sure to inform your doctor of the problem and the treatment as soon as possible, especially if medication has been prescribed. Don't assume that the doctor on call will relate this information to your doctor.

☐ Memorize the telephone numbers of your pediatrician, hospital, ambulance, and poison control center. It only takes a few minutes.

☐ If your child is sick and you're going to call the doctor about it, make sure you write down the child's temperature and symptoms and the questions you want to ask. Nothing's worse than hanging up and remembering another question. Also, write down what the doctor says: Quite often you're so rattled that you'll just agree with the doctor and promptly forget the details of the instructions. (See CALLING THE DOCTOR, p. 217.)

☐ If your baby has a fever, a thermometer in the rectum will register it quickly—within ten or twenty seconds. If the mercury doesn't move from around 98.6° or 99° by that time, release the baby. It takes only about thirty seconds to get a fairly accurate rectal temperature—that is, within one degree of accuracy. The books that tell you to leave the thermometer in for three minutes have *never* dealt with a screaming, squirming baby. You do that only if your doctor asks for an *exact* temperature.

☐ One mother offered the following: *"I really feel it helps a child who's sick to have calm parents. Even if you're scared to death inside, try to be calm and soothe the baby."*

☐ Use unbreakable thermometers if you're traveling and your baby gets sick.

☐ Put a key (or any small, cold metal object) on the back of baby's neck to stop nosebleeds.

☐ Keep a gel-filled plastic cold pack in your freezer at all times for emergency use. In a pinch, almost any small item from your freezer, wrapped in a soft cloth, can act as a cold compress.

☐ If you must administer a compress and baby struggles, try

to get her to hold it herself. She might make a mess of it, but at least she'll get the job done.

☐ Remove adhesive bandages easily by rubbing them with baby oil first. This only works with the perforated bandages, though. Soak others off in the bath.

☐ If you're trying to keep children with colds away from your baby and they don't get the message, tell them your baby is sick and you don't want *them* to catch it.

Pediatricians

☐ When you interview a pediatrician, you're really looking for the personal rapport and trust that is so necessary in any doctor/patient relationship. You might be charged for an office interview; check the doctor's policy beforehand. Here are some points that you should discuss:

- Hospital affiliation
- Medical background: school attended, any specialities
- How long she/he has been in practice
- The schedule of visits (How often is the baby seen in the first year?)
- Interest in and support of breast feeding (or any other specific interest you may have)
- The backup support (Who covers when she/he is away?)
- For your nonemergency-type questions about baby, is there a special time for patients to call? Does the nurse or the doctor handle these?
- Visits after hours
- House calls

- Doctor's policy about prescribing medicine over the phone without an office visit
- Their ideas about solid foods and when they should be started
- Their own children, if any
- Their method of examination (Is the baby undressed by the parent or the nurse? Can the parent hold the baby during most of the exam? This prevents a lot of crying.).

☐ If you are unhappy with your pediatrician *do not hesitate to change*. Many parents are reluctant to do this because they feel their pediatrician "knows" their baby. One has to realize that another doctor can get to "know" a baby very quickly. It is so important for children and parents to feel comfortable and secure with their pediatrician. If you decide to change pediatricians, do let the doctor or a member of the staff know your reason for leaving. This is a form of constructive criticism and is important feedback for the doctor.

☐ Call your doctor *whenever you have a question*. That's what doctors are there for. Don't feel shy about inundating him or her with questions, no matter how trivial they may seem. You and your child deserve answers.

☐ If your pediatrician is unavailable and there is no backup service, call the emergency room at your nearest hospital and find out whether someone on duty can help you.

☐ Many areas of the country now have doctors available for making house calls (remember house calls?). Check your phone directory to see whether a doctor house-call service is available in your area. Use these services only when absolutely necessary.

⊐ Use the form supplied on p. 217 for recording the information you'll need to give your doctor when you speak with him or her.

Taking Medicine

⊐ Put it in baby's food, milk, or juice *if* your doctor approves. Or, as you're feeding her, just squirt it on her spoon and pop it in.

⊐ If baby refuses to take medicine from you, he might take it from someone else, like your husband or mother.

⊐ Pretend to give it to an older sibling first.

⊐ Try a syringe. Squirt the medicine in the side of the mouth and hold it closed.

⊐ Babies will take medicine without a fuss if they know you mean to give it to them no matter what.

⊐ Generic brands of aspirin are every bit as good as name brands—and a lot cheaper.

⊐ One baby aspirin is the equivalent of one-quarter of an adult aspirin.

⊐ Never administer medicine in the dark.

⊐ Never give a baby an old prescription for a new illness.

⊐ When administering eardrops, warm the bottle first by placing it in a pan of warm water for a few minutes.

⊐ Be sure to keep medications in the refrigerator if the instructions so indicate.

⊐ The large medicine droppers and/or special spoons you

can buy at the pharmacy are *much* better than regular
spoons for administering medicine.

Colds and Congestion

☐ Elevate one end of the crib mattress so that baby's head
will be raised. This helps baby breathe. If you can't hook
the mattress support onto the next level hook, stuff a
blanket under it, or put a thick book under each forward
leg to raise the end of the crib.

☐ A mild salt-and-water solution gently dropped on the nose
mucus will loosen it. Ask your doctor for the exact
proportion of salt to water. Also, try putting a dab of
petroleum jelly under baby's nose to soothe and protect.

☐ Use a nasal syringe to gently remove some of the mucus.

☐ Moist air in the room helps. Use a humidifier or vaporizer.
Humidifiers seem safer because there's no need to boil
water, but they can cause the air to cool, so be sure to
compensate for any heat loss.

☐ If your baby is very congested and having trouble breathing, steam up the bathroom by running the hot water in
the shower for a few minutes. Keep baby in the bathroom,
playing with a toy, for a while. Do not leave baby alone in
the bathroom.

☐ If your baby has a cold but no fever, do not give aspirin. It
doesn't help a cold, and nosebleeds may develop.

Diarrhea

☐ Diarrhea in babies is serious. They dehydrate very quickly. Call your doctor at the first sign of it.

☐ If your child is dehydrated from vomiting or diarrhea and won't take liquids, put him in the bathtub with the water running. Cup your hands to catch some water and let him drink the water from your hands. Your baby will think this is a terrific game and will soon begin to drink from his own hands.

☐ Watch for diarrhea patterns—for example, after baby eats certain foods, or when teething.

☐ You'll probably hear it from your doctor: Rice cereal and bananas is good for babies with diarrhea when they want to start eating again.

☐ Substitute rice water (water that rice has boiled in) for plain water when your baby has diarrhea.

☐ Get your baby to take a pinch of salt to avoid dehydration. The salt, of course, won't help the dehydration problem, but it will make her thirsty, and she'll drink more liquids.

Babies in Hospitals

☐ There's depression and lots of anger when your baby is in the hospital. Your marriage can suffer from the pressure. Each parent is reluctant to add to the other's burden, so you don't talk about it. This isn't good. Talk to each other, or get help from a social worker or therapist if there's a real problem. Because your baby needs you, you have to be in the best shape possible.

YOUR CHILD'S
IMMUNIZATION CHART AND HEALTH RECORD

Child's Name _____

IMMUNIZATION		
Recommended Age	**For**	**Date of Immunization or Visit**
2 months	DTP	
	Diphtheria, tetanus	
	Pertussis (whooping cough)	
	OVP	
	Oral polio vaccine	
4 months	DTP, OPV	
6 months	DTP, OPV	
12 months	Tuberculin skin test	
(or by 1 year)	(test for tuberculosis)	
15 months	MMR	
	Measles, mumps,	
	rubella (German measles)	
18 months	DTP, OPV (booster)	
4-6 years	DTP, OPV (booster)	
14-16 years	TD	
	Tetanus, diphtheria (booster)	

VISITS TO DOCTOR

Height	Weight	Comments, illness, treatment	Doctor

☐ Try to be patient with your spouse; people grieve in different ways. Don't be misled by a relaxed, positive attitude. Any parent whose child is ill is suffering.

☐ From about three or four months on, your baby really needs you there in the hospital. The nurses try their best, but they're busy, and anyway, baby needs and wants *you*.

☐ Mothers and fathers should alternate spending nights in the hospital with baby, so both can get some rest.

☐ Accept with gratitude any help from family and friends. Hire someone to do as much cooking and cleaning as you can afford. You're under enough strain without extra chores.

Babies in Casts

☐ You'll spare yourself some grief if you realize that babies under five months don't mind casts on their legs. In fact, they don't seem to be bothered by them at all. The three-month-old son of one mother we talked with learned to bang the casts against the infant seat and make a terrible racket. He loved it.

☐ Rub some petroleum jelly on the edges of the cast to avoid skin irritations and chafing.

☐ To bathe a baby with casts on her legs, put plastic bags over the casts, and then lower her into a little water in a baby bathtub. Leave the legs hanging over the side so they won't get wet.

☐ To remove casts on baby's legs, put a little vinegar in the water you soak them in. The casts come off in record time. Also, it really helps if two people tackle this job together. One person holds baby; the other fiddles with the casts.

16

As Your Baby Grows

An Alternative to Saying "No"

☐ At some point, it seems as if all you say to your child is "No!" even if you've baby-proofed the house so well you can hardly live in it. Figure out some *positive* things to say instead, like "Hot!," "Pet the cat *this* way," "Share your toys," "Spit it out—it tastes bad!" This way of speaking does not come naturally, by the way. It's learned behavior.

☐ When the only thing your child says is "no," it means *you*'ve been saying it too much.

Around the House

☐ If your baby can't quite sit by himself, wedge him in the corner of a big box, put some toys inside, and he'll play happily.

☐ Babies just learning to sit up should always be surrounded by pillows or soft toys.

☐ If you live in a bilevel home, don't bring small items upstairs each time you need to. Keep a basket at the foot of the stairs and throw the items into it. Bring the basket upstairs once or twice a day.

☐ If your child insists on watching TV four inches away from the screen (most children do), introduce a special TV seat—a baby rocker, a booster seat, a piece of old carpeting, a pillow—anything to draw her farther away from the TV.

☐ To prevent a child in a walker from falling over every time he hits a raised doorway threshold, tape strips of cardboard over the bump to act as a gentle ramp.

☐ *Always* set a timer when you've got something on the stove. Babies are so distracting, and it's so easy to forget!

☐ Keep an "outgrown clothing basket" in baby's room and deposit appropriate articles into it. Launder and store these things separately.

☐ Put up a bulletin board in baby's room and use it as a "clearing center" for single socks, stray toy parts, medication schedules, "firsts" that you want to enter in your baby book when you have time, baby's immunization schedule, birthday cards, pictures of relatives who are far away, and anything else you can think of!

Changing Baby's Habits

☐ If you and your spouse feel you must try to change your baby's behavior, then decide together on a plan, stick to it, and use each other for mutual support.

☐ If you're going to try something new with baby (like weaning or breaking a night-time awakening habit), decide how long you're going to stick with it—a week, four days, or whatever. (Four days is a minimum tryout period.) Time limits relieve the pressure of wondering whether to stop or to continue a course of action.

☐ Whenever you want to try to change something, *you* have to be ready. It's not enough for someone else to say "You should let him cry if he wakes up at night" or "Just don't give him the pacifier." You must feel that what you're doing is right—for you *and* the baby. Then it will usually work. If you have *any* doubt, baby will sense it.

☐ Babies' habits and schedules change rapidly. Just as you've worked out a successful routine, baby changes. Be alert and be flexible.

THE PACIFIER: GIVING IT UP

☐ Keep in mind that if the child really needs to suck, he'll probably resort to his thumbs. You might have to decide what sucking habit is least offensive to you and go from there.

☐ Try cutting a small hole in the pacifier or otherwise altering its shape. One mother said, *"I cut some sticky stuff off my son's pacifier, and the minute I put it back in his mouth, he spit it out. He's never touched it again."*

☐ Dip pacifier in pickle juice (or anything that's unpleasant but not harmful), and soon baby won't want it anymore.

☐ When your child gives up the pacifier, she may also give up naps and have more trouble getting to sleep. Take your choice.

Crawling and Walking Babies

☐ To teach baby to crawl backwards downstairs, just keep turning her around until she gets the idea. But always supervise babies on stairs or close the gates.

☐ If your child can stand but doesn't know how to sit, you'd better teach him, or he'll scream for you or fall straight backwards when he's tired of standing. Bend one knee and then the other to get him to squat and sit on his fanny. It might take anywhere from two hours to two days, but if you persist, baby will learn.

Security Blankets

☐ Keep a cloth diaper near baby and in bed at all times. If she does need a "security blanket" and chooses the diaper, you'll be very lucky. It's small, soft, and inconspicuous—and you can replace it when needed with a clean one.

☐ Try to buy at least two of whatever your child chooses as a security blanket so you always have a spare when one is being laundered.

Teething

☐ Be careful with *any* food you give your baby for teething. Some babies really go after it and break off hunks that they might choke on. You know your baby—just choose carefully and supervise. Many brands of teething biscuits contain a lot of sugar. Before you buy them, consider some good alternatives (once again, be careful when offering your baby any food on which she may possibly choke):

- The knuckle of your index finger
- A frozen pacifier
- A small washcloth (It can be chilled.)
- A little Scotch (bourbon, etc.) rubbed on the gums with your finger or a cotton swab
- The hard part of a melon rind (cool and tasty)
- Hard, stale whole wheat toast cut into narrow strips (easy to hold and nutritious)
- Thin strips of broiled steak (use tough pieces)
- Frozen bagels (cool, and they don't crumble)
- Cold vegetables (carrots, broccoli stems)
- Ice pops (You can make these yourself with fruit juice.)

☐ Keep babies going places and doing things so they won't be as aware of the pain. In other words, distract them!

Grooming

☐ Cut baby's nails while she's tired or sleeping. Use baby scissors made especially for this purpose.

☐ Cut baby's hair when it's dry or it might wind up uneven. To cut bangs evenly, place a strip of adhesive tape across (while hair is dry), then cut.

☐ In summer, cut baby's hair outdoors so you won't have to worry about the mess.

☐ Haircuts are safer and faster when two people tackle the job. One amuses or holds the baby while the other cuts.

☐ Visits to the barber will be less of an ordeal if you let your baby sit in your lap while his hair is being cut.

☐ Don't put a mirror in front of your baby when you cut his hair. It looks scary to most kids!

☐ Invest in a pair of haircutting scissors. They're sharper and will result in a better cut.

☐ Clean baby's teeth with a gauze pad onto which you have rubbed a small amount of toothpaste.

Preserving Your Memories

☐ An instant-developing camera is invaluable for capturing the moment (that first step!) that will never come again. And you'll know immediately if the picture came out.

☐ Take home movies only when there are few people present. Chaos results if too many people get involved. The simpler, the better. Get a sound camera if you can afford it.

☐ Always date your pictures (with the year, too). If you're taking sound movies, announce the date as you start to shoot.

☐ Always keep an extra roll of film at home.

☐ Take pictures of the baby from *his* eye level.

☐ Buy a baby book you *really* like. If you're given one that you don't particularly care for, get your own instead. You'll probably be more inclined to work on the book if it's one you really love.

☐ A tree planted in your yard the year of baby's birth will be a wonderful thing to share with your child as she grows.

☐ Bronzed baby shoes are still popular, but if your taste is more modern, have your baby's shoes preserved in a clear acrylic block. Or, if you want to handle the project yourself, consider painting the shoe with thick coats of an oil-base paint. Paint on designs and baby's name in a contrasting color. The result is a lovely paperweight or "vase" for dried flowers.

Important Telephone Numbers

Keep copies of this list, with the phone numbers filled in, at *each* telephone extension in your home.

Pediatrician_____

Ob/gyn_____

Family doctor_____

Drugstore_____

Mother's business_____

Father's business_____

Friends and

neighbors_____

_____

_____

_____

_____

Police_____

Fire_____

Ambulance_____

Poison control center_____

Hospital_____

Calling the Doctor

Make copies of this page and fill it in before you call the doctor. If you keep the forms, you'll have a good record of your child's illnesses.

INFORMATION TO HAVE READY:

Age of child: _____

Weight of child: _____

Temperature
(indicate whether it is
rectal or axillary): _____

SYMPTOMS: (vomiting, _____
watery eyes, etc.) _____

Sequence and duration _____
of symptoms: _____

APPEARANCE: (pale, _____
flushed, spotted, etc.) _____

Location and exact _____
appearance of any _____
rash: _____

TREATMENT OR _____
MEDICINE ADMIN- _____
ISTERED BEFORE _____
CALLING (aspirin, anti- _____
histamine, etc.): _____

QUESTIONS TO ASK: _____

_____

DOCTOR'S INSTRUCTIONS:

_____

_____

_____

Keep these completed sheets in a file and you'll be able to refer to them whenever it becomes necessary.

My Own Tips: What Worked for Me

Use this space for recording your own special tips. In addition, feel free, as you use this book, to write in it often, indicating which tips worked best for you. This annotated copy will come in useful later on with other children, or it will make a unique gift for you to hand on to another new parent.

Know a Great Tip?

If you have a tip that would make another parent's life easier, please send it to us for future editions of this book.

Just send to:

Brooke McKamy Beebe
c/o Dell Trade Paperbacks
1 Dag Hammarskjold Plaza
New York, New York 10017

Sending your tips constitutes your permission for accepted tips to be used in any edition of *Best Bets for Babies*.

Index